THE BRIDES OF CHRIST

World Wide Conspiracy | Vol. 1

by
Valetta Johnson

Gotham Books

30 N Gould St.
Ste. 20820, Sheridan, WY 82801
https://gothambooksinc.com/

Phone: 1 (307) 464-7800

© 2024 *Valetta Johnson*. All rights reserved.

No part of this book may be reproduced, stored in a retrieval system, or transmitted by any means without the written permission of the author.

Published by Gotham Books (May 8, 2024)

ISBN: 979-8-88775-718-6 (P)
ISBN: 979-8-88775-719-3 (E)

Because of the dynamic nature of the Internet, any web addresses or links contained in this book may have changed since publication and may no longer be valid.

The views expressed in this work are solely those of the author and do not necessarily reflect the views of the publisher, and the publisher hereby disclaims any responsibility for them.

Table of Contents

ACKNOWLEDGMENT IV
PREFACE V
INTRODUCTION IX
CHAPTER 1 TRIALS OF GROWING UP 1
CHAPTER 2 MOVING ON 39
CHAPTER 3 BEWILDERED YET BELOVED 64
CHAPTER 4 A DIFFERENT HORIZON 97
CHAPTER 5 WELCOMED ADDITION 138
CHAPTER 6 MOVING DIDN'T MATTER 153
CHAPTER 7 ONE THING LED TO ANOTHER 169
CHAPTER 8 FAMILY TIES 190
CHAPTER 9 BEING A LIVING TESTIMONY 208
APPENDIX 244

Acknowledgment

I would like to thank God for giving me the direction that he gave, to show me in his word, that his word was like a manual for our life's and without him or his word, this mission never would have been completed. I also appreciate the fact that he manages to resolve the issues with my mother, and she eventually became the mother that I could call on. God was my mother, when there was nowhere else to turn. And first and foremost, my Lord and Savior Jesus Christ, who died that all people would experience the grace that would allow all women a better chance at preparing for their family.

Preface

When this author's tumultuous journey led her life through a couple of rapes and a justifiable homicide, not to mention other encounters her life survived, she felt as Moses once did and became. Yet she was determined to live a normal life even though the author wanted nothing more than to live a normal life. The world was watching and waiting to hear her testimony since she was triumphant in her will to rise above the odds. She stayed busy as an entrepreneur and workaholic. Even though she had always wanted to share her experience, she didn't know when or where it would happen. Since it was such a sensitive matter, the author decided to move on in life.

Many that knew of the author suspected she was a spiritual person because of the crosses she would wear, thinking they were her good-luck charms, but the author had a deeper relationship with God than most people knew, including herself.

It wasn't until she realized that God was calling her into the ministry and understanding what a calling was made her thankful to God for a chance to fulfill her destiny in him. When she answered the calling on her life is when everything began to make sense, and she realized how she lived through the good and the bad things in life to help others to find their strength in God as she had.

The author wasn't open to share everything in her life... until she ended up going to a church where she had to confront the abortion issue, opening another can of worms. Now this meant she would have to face the demons that called abortion murder as well, and this meant she would have to dig up her past and find peace with the abortion she had. That made it even more difficult to share with others openly.

Since others knew of her battles, and others were just curious, she knew she had to set the records straight and give the Lord the glory. This is how the book came into play.

As she attempted to write the book, reservations arose as she contemplated sharing about the abortion and how she started to name the book "Sin for a Season," yet it wasn't her intention to glorify sin because most of us are in situations where sin has dominated our lives, and her life was no different than others.

After coming to terms on sharing about the abortion, the author felt the truth would set her free, and she would have to depend on the leading of the Lord since she also felt the abortion was a blessing in disguise because the pregnancy would've been untimely.

As the author struggled for acceptance in the church, she knew it wasn't going to happen unless she lowered her standards and agreed with the hypocrites of the world. Nevertheless, it wasn't an option; the author couldn't agree with the traditional churches, and she opted to separate herself from that church doctrine and sought the face of God directly.

Her journey through the Bible fascinates her. As she dissects the Bible, her awareness unveils the deepest, darkest secrets of the Bible and exposes the Antichrist. And then she stumbles upon a book that reaches out and touches her, with only a revelation that she can reveal: Second John, "The Elect Lady." As she reads this book, it becomes evident that she is this lady, and the book was written for her.

Suddenly, her life is an open book before the actual book is written—as the government precariously watches and guards her every move, until her life is everything but normal. She knows now that she must save many with her testimony before it's too late. The spirit of the Antichrist has filled the world with lies and deception, but the truth will come through the Word of God and her testimony.

Throughout the Bible, the author is inspired as she identifies with the Ethiopian daughter's testimony and imagines herself as this lady, yet the Antichrist is trying to come against her at her job, home, and the church of Satan. Now the author knows that, for such a time as now, her life has been preserved to expose the Antichrist and save the world from ultimate doom.

While the presidents ignored her warnings, the judgment of God swept over America, and it may not be over yet. It took the author three years to write the book because she didn't start writing the book until she answered God's calling on her life and her refusal to believe that the abortion issue had to be dealt with by the entire world. Then it took fifteen years to get the book published because many refused to believe the truth in God's Word. After the pandemic in 2020, the book was revised because it put an entirely new spin on the book.

Introduction

An autobiography that took a utopia turn, this book is written in the third-person form by the author, and the names have been changed to protect those identified in the book, especially the author.

A young lady struggled in her teen years to find herself established and independent before making a commitment to God while growing up in a dysfunctional family environment. She knew nothing was going to be given to her on a silver platter, and she would have gladly worked for it.

Despite her desire to become independent, she held her own in God as she attempted to be a witness in a worldly way. Some thought she was a child prodigy until she proved that she was much more, after buying her first home after high school, only to encounter numerous burglaries. However, after her life was threatened by a rapist, the author was forced to purchase a gun. Most people would have moved long before the rape, but even then, she was determined to hold on to a home, which she never had as a child. And after moving from one place to another growing up, she was determined not to let them drive her away from her home.

Nine months after the first rape, another attempt on her life proved deadly for another rapist as she defended herself and killed the rapist on his way out the door.

She becomes a local hero despite knowing that she did nothing herself, but God's strength and courage pulled her through. Even though the author realized that God alone had carried her through the countless trials her life had already experienced, she still couldn't come to terms with going to church, knowing that she didn't want to be a hypocrite; she prayed and studied about God in her own way.

Eventually, the enemy lured her sister into the drug world and cost her sister her life. Being extremely close to this sister, it became the straw that broke the camel's back since it was her sister's husband's drug involvement that led the author down the wrong road as well. After the burial of her sister, the author's life was resurrected.

Finally, her decision to join the church took on an adventure and fun-filled journey as she committed to the things of God, and she then realized what a calling was. She became the living testimony that she had prayed her sister would be. Directions into prison ministry led her to minister to the man that killed her sister, and he began to preach in the prison.

Her life became full of church activities. As she taught the four- and five-year-olds, she was teaching herself as well. It was a need in the church everywhere she turned; missions and joining the choir had the author busy from sunup until sundown until her growth was stumped, then magnified, by the abortion issue. It seemed like her passion to know and love God made her question another phase of the church that encouraged pregnant girls to adopt out their babies to the church.

The author didn't feel condemned by the abortion she experienced at the age of seventeen; as a matter of fact, she felt thankful that they had legal abortion at the time, and she didn't want to be a hypocrite with the issue, especially since the church had become a welfare system promoting sin.

Also, the minister saying malicious things about abortion to try to condemn women from having one made the author leery. Since the minister was single, he knew that a lot of women were there for him, and the author also sensed he was trying to flirt with her. For that reason, she let the man of God know that if God ever called her to minister in the abortion area, the only thing she could do was pray that God would direct their decision.

After the author informed the minister of her views on abortion, she was glad that she got it off her chest, and she was ready to move on, but it wasn't that easy. One thing led to another, and before she knew it, it seemed like the signs were leading the author to defend women that needed an abortion; however, it wouldn't be at the church she was at since they wanted to kick her out of the church after the letter the author wrote and all the other things, she did prove to her point.

Obedience was the furthest thing on her mind when she realized how many would oppose her. Even the women's movement was annoyed by her when she tried to stand by the Word of God. Finally, her only defense was the Bible as the author studied to show herself approved, rightfully dividing the Word of God. More evidence in the Bible proved that the false teachers had misled the churches and that the government might have helped them.

As she stood by the Word of God, amazingly, near the end of the Bible, John wrote a book to the elect lady. To her surprise, it seemed like the book bore witness with her spirit. She began to feel an awesome connection with the book, especially since her name tied in with the book. The author knew the word *children* also referred to all the believers that agreed with this truth, but the scary thing about it was John warned her that those opposing the choices for women were the Antichrist.

Now the author knows that some people don't know they are the Antichrist, and she needs to show them in the Bible. One book led to another book titled: *"Forbidden Fruit"*. The author would like to challenge the atheists and help people understand the scriptures and how to read the Bible.

Ironically, John also wrote, in 3 John, to Gaius, a disciple of Jesus Christ, how to beware of the opposer of Christ. He described in this book exactly what happened at the first church that the author attended; even the minister's name was identified in this book as an arrogant and stubborn leader of the Gospel. John warned Gaius, for the love of God, not to take anything from the Gentiles because he needed to teach the people the right way of truth.

The author believes that these two books at the end of the Bible prove that the abortion issue has been around for a long time, and mostly all the books in the Bible refer to it one way or the other. However scary it may seem, when God talked about illegitimacy in the Old Testament, and then also in the New Testament, he didn't change his law, yet our society has polluted the world with a different standard, creating a diversion on the face of the earth. Yet God has blessed our country with the diversity of many offsprings, but truth must prevail. When we see what's going on in China, and our country still seems ignorant to the pure facts, it's time to get real.

Chapter 1

Trials of Growing Up

The crackling whispers sounded, and the aroma of fire sizzled as the parents alerted the others that something was terribly wrong.

Papa Joseph Johnson raced through the house, grabbing the little ones as the older daughter gathered herself and ran out the front door where Mother was waiting with high hopes that all would be saved.

Papa Joseph, scorched and battered, came out with the two youngest girls in his arms while James, the oldest, had the two younger boys. Josie, the eldest girl, had clinched on to Mother. Now they all huddled together as the firemen came. You could hear the sirens blast in the distance.

All six children were accounted for and at the nick of time; it seemed like the roof was caving in from the fire, leaving the house in utter ashes as the neighbors gathered around to offer their help. At 2:00 in the morning, it was a bit cold.

The January cold had settled in, in Northern Oklahoma. It was not always a sunny climate, and when it was cold, it was cold. Mother and Father held each other in despair, knowing their problems would be easier to deal with since they were together.

Just then, the firemen arrived and began to finish what was left of the smoldering fire. While Papa gave a report to the police officer, one of the neighbors offered Mother and the children a place to camp until it was over. It looked like all of them got out with just the clothes on their backs, and that was about it. They would have to start over, from having a place to stay to having clothes to put on their backs, but it seemed better just knowing they were family.

After Papa came in from talking with the officer, he told the others that the police officer suspected someone caught the house on fire because of the evidence they found in the back of the house. Mother was upset, wondering who could have done this and not caring about the family.

As they pondered on what enemies surrounded them, they just grew weary and decided to give it to God, knowing that he would protect them from all harm. Papa still had a job and needed it more than ever now, so he didn't sleep much that night, but a wink here and there.

At daybreak, Mother and Papa were agreeing on what they had planned to do that day since they knew they didn't want to burden the neighbors any longer than they had.

A family of eight was now without shelter, clothing, and food. Papa had planned on going to work and asking about getting some time off because of this situation. Papa had a sister who was dear and near to him, and she was always able to help, and Mom's mother was always there to extend a helping hand. Papa worked at the City Refuse Department, and even though it was hauling trash, he was glad to have a job to support his family.

That evening, Papa came home with good news—his job took up an offering, and the church where they attended frequently did the same thing. Papa had already started looking for another place to live. It seemed like offerings and services were pouring in, and clothes were donated as well. Papa's sister worked at a laundromat, and she found a lot of clothing that was left behind. She knew the lost-and-found was never claimed most of the time, and if someone came back looking for anything, she would just tell them they were donated. Within a week, the family had settled in their new place, and the donations and offerings as well as those that gave to the cause, were blessings they could thank God for.

The Johnson were no more than the typical American family that struggled in a society that often neglected the needs of the poor people, but the community pulled together and helped one another. As a strong tower rose, they rose to the occasion, and now, the kids were back in school, and Mother tended to the younger ones at home until they were able to attend school.

Even though Papa's grandfather was a street preacher, it was Mother who was adamant about taking the children to church. Now that the older children were back in school, Mother kept herself busy with the two younger girls, Candi and Babe. As they played together, it seemed like they fussed more than anything. As Babe went around singing and praising the Lord, Mother had a feeling that she would be the one that would enjoy church. Babe was very impressionable, and it seemed like she liked to think that God and his angels were always looking after them. Mother couldn't remember exactly if it was when the house burned down when Babe habitually started talking about the Lord.

Babe's obsession to know God and be about the church business also came because of Mother being involved in the Pentecostal Church while she was pregnant with Babe. Babe was the last of seven children, although the oldest brother wasn't from the same mother. Now the Johnson attended a more traditional church, but they switched over to Baptist after Babe was born. Babe found herself in church even when others had no desire or interest to attend.

Babe had such a tear-jerking experience when a preview of Jesus's Crucifixion was shown at the church. She wanted more than anything, to be involved with the church's Easter pageant.

She felt that it was her way of giving something back to Jesus. After Babe asked her mother if it was okay, with Mother's approval, Babe received a speech from the director of the pageant. Babe studied and recited it; she was overwhelmed with joy to be able to participate.

All eyes were on Babe as she stepped up to the microphone and loudly proclaimed her love for the Lord Jesus and denounced sin in her life as she would live for the Lord. At the tender age of seven, Babe didn't know what sin was, but she knew that was what her speech said, which she had remembered. As she exited the stage, all stood for a standing ovation, and at the reception, Mother was proud to see her little angel perform as well as she did.

It seemed like Babe was fondest of the church, and it wasn't long before she signed up for water baptism. Papa was too busy working, but the other children were there to witness, even if they didn't feel compelled to follow her leadings, and it never was pushed on any of them because Mother felt that she couldn't force such a decision on her children.

But with Babe, it seemed natural. As Babe bubbled around with her newfound faith, her brothers were always there to defend her. They all tried to look after their sisters, but by now, everyone in school was struggling with something since Papa and Mother never completed high school themselves. It took some real studying to overcome the obstacles and challenges that school was bringing. James and Josie as well as Martin and Joseph Jr. (who was called JJ since he was named after Papa) were busy at studying for school and helping with the family chores.

Josie combed Candi's and Babe's hair and cared for the two girls after Mother found a job at a department store. It seemed like the busier Papa and Mother stayed working to put food on the table, the more distance took over, which slipped right in, and separation issues became so settled because everyone was busy in their own world.

By now, Candi and Babe were in school, and that gave Mother a chance to find a job and help with the family responsibilities; it also gave the kids more time to get involved in mischief after school, which would eventually cause trouble.

After school one evening, while everyone was taking turns riding the only bike they had, JJ offered to take Babe for a ride—that way, she didn't have to wait as long. They had learned how to saddle up with Babe on the handlebars while JJ peddled. JJ had taken a liking to cruising down Roosevelt Hills, a hilly elite district with lots of trees and shrubs. As they struggled up the hills, JJ knew that downhill would be a breeze because he had done it several times. Down the hill, he peddled at first, but then the speed was so enormous he didn't have to peddle at all. It seemed like they automatically glided at an increasingly high speed while the wind pushed them forward. The breeze kept them refreshed until, suddenly, JJ forgot the stop sign, and it would've tossed Babe overboard. Yet the car coming from the opposite direction couldn't avoid the crash that threw Babe in a hedge of bushes while for JJ, screeching brakes couldn't save him from the impact of the car crashing into him.

As the couple got out of the car, Babe was dusting herself off the pile of leaves she had fallen into. The couple was amazed at how she didn't show any signs that she was hurt, but it was obvious that JJ was, as they scrapped their bike off the side of the curve. They gently picked up JJ, but it seemed like the only thing wrong was his leg was broken. They immediately gathered them both in their car and proceeded to go to the hospital, where they called their parents while JJ got his leg casted.

Papa and Mother were there about the same time JJ finished getting his leg casted. The couple was nice enough to wait and meet the parents, and boy, was Mother upset. She wanted to start whipping JJ there, but since he had a cast on his leg, she held off, but she promised him a good whooping after he recovered. She didn't even have to ask how Babe got there since JJ was the oldest. But she was thankful that Babe didn't have a scar on her from the accident. After that incident, it seemed like Papa and Mother just knew Babe was a trooper and God had his hands on her.

School wasn't a big hit in the Johnson family. Babe wasn't crazy about school like her other brothers and sisters; she struggled with studying. Babe ended up being put in special education while she was in elementary school, but for some reason it was just to guard her from being bullied. Nevertheless, Babe's teacher saw some potential in Babe even when she didn't study. Babe's teacher wanted her to sign up for the spelling bee. Babe didn't really want to, but she was elected anyway.

Babe never studied for it, and she didn't even look forward to it, maybe because no one in the family showed any interest. The teacher was upset with Babe when she missed a simple word like *chimney*. She couldn't believe it, but Babe tried not to take it personally when she lost because she didn't want to enter, but the teacher made her. Then the teacher realized that Babe wasn't getting enough encouragement from home, but she knew that she couldn't follow her home.

As Babe began to blossom her baby fat got in the way of her maturity, and with Josie wearing a bra now, Babe thought that she needed one also. Her baby fat left her chubby and jolly. Babe tried on Josie's bra. She could tell it was kind of big, but she didn't care; she just wanted to cover herself up. That evening, Babe was anxious to go to the store with Papa, and boy was he surprised to see Babe in a bra. Papa joked about her rushing things as he looked down at her bra. Babe still only in the third grade explained to Papa that she was too fat, and she thought she needed a bra. Papa explained that it was only baby fat. Babe was still awfully bashful, and that night, when they returned from the store and before she went to bed, she remembered praying to God: "Please, God, don't let them get too big."

Babe and Candi both struggled with baby fat, and Candi worried that she would be a diabetic. She would remember everything she had eaten that day, and at the end of the day, she would ask James, the oldest brother if eating all she had eaten would make her a diabetic, and James would assure her that it wouldn't. Yet they continued growing like normal girls, and while the others prepared for high school, others were held back in school because of lack of understanding. Out of the six children, three were held back while the others barely made it through the system.

Despite the setbacks in the family, they still managed through life even though some were held back a year because the teacher noticed some deficiencies in their ability to learn. It made Babe study a bit more, but it seemed like there were still things that kept her from focusing.

It became more apparent when Papa and Mother began to fight more and stories of infidelity hit the surface, next came the divorce. It seemed like Josie and James were more prepared for it than the others; they had taken on the role as the oldest, and they knew what to expect, but it didn't seem real to Babe because she just knew God could fix anything, but finally, Babe had to accept it. She found herself in her prayer closet, hoping that God would save her family, but when reality set in, Babe knew that it would be better if they went their own separate ways for them to be happy. By now, Babe was not a child anymore; she had grown up fast enough to accept what was going on in her life.

With the separation going on, Mother moved the children with her at her mother's place, where she would stay until the divorce was final. Grandmother was glad to receive Mother and all the children, even if the house was too small. Granny made a way for them all to be fed, clothed, and taken care of. Granny wasn't fond of Papa, and she resented the fact that she had to make him marry Mother when she got pregnant with James, to hear about a shotgun wedding. This shocked Babe because she knew nothing of it until they moved in with Granny. Now that Papa and Mother were divorcing, Granny didn't hold back telling him how she felt about him, and all this time, Babe thought they had the best family.

Now to find out that Papa and Mother stayed in the relationship over ten years even though they were forced to get married just proved to Babe that even forcing them to marry didn't assure them it would work, but they had five more children after that.

Mother was the second of two daughters that Granny had. Her sister lived in Texas now, but she had a house in Tulsa that she was trying to sell, and since it wasn't sold yet, Granny agreed that Mother should move into it after the divorce was final. Mother thought it was a good idea, but Aunt Etta's house was small as well. Candi liked staying with Granny because she was named after Granny, and Babe was named after her mother's sister, Juanetta.

They just called her Babe because her papa started with that nickname, and she never outgrew it. James was named after one of Granny's boyfriends, and Joseph was named after Papa. Martin just ended up with his name, and Josie was also named after Papa.

That summer, the family moved into Aunt Etta's empty house—another adjustment to make. The neighborhood was settled, with a few children around the corner. It didn't seem very social, especially after finding out that one of the neighbors did hair in her home and one of her frequent customers was Papa's new girlfriend, much to Mother's surprise.

One day when Papa's new girlfriend was getting her hair done, the brothers found out and told their mother. She had one of the boys tell the lady that she wanted to talk with her after she finished with her hair. Mrs. Bird was Papa's new girlfriend, and it wasn't until later that Papa started bringing her over to see the kids, but whatever Mrs. Bird and Mother talked about that day wasn't kids' business. Babe didn't know if her mom didn't want her to date her father or what; Mrs. Bird didn't carry on as she was upset, but Mom did. Sometimes, it just seemed like adults can be stupid. Babe didn't know how to tell her mother to leave the nice lady alone without getting scorned herself. Babe questioned that if Mother was mad at Papa, she should take it out on him instead of the lady. Nevertheless, it seemed like after that, the neighborhood wasn't going to be a big hit.

With school about to start, they were preparing for the best even if it did seem like the worst. Josie and James, the two eldest weren't around much. James stayed with Granny to help her out, and Josie stayed with Paula, a dear friend of Mother's. Candi and Babe always found things to separate them, but when Papa came by, they would always find a way to be together. Papa started a tradition: right before school started, he would take them out to buy school supplies—notebooks, papers, pens, etc.

Papa started living with his girlfriend right after they all met her, and since they lived in some newly built projects that were much larger than Aunt Etta's home.

Joseph and Martin stayed with Papa most of the time. Mrs. Bird had two sons of her own and a daughter. At times, Candi and Babe would stay the weekend and hang out with Ester, her daughter. Ester was younger than both, but they didn't notice the difference. Since Ester was the only girl in her family, she was glad to know Candi and Babe.

Papa worked on cars on the side, and Joseph and Martin took an interest in cars as well; however, the auto-mechanic course they took turned out to be more than they could handle—neither one of them were doing very well, and this gave Mother a chance to meet the teacher, Mr. Black, who turned out to be more than just a teacher. Before long, it seemed like Mother and Mr. Black had some kind of love connection going on, and whatever was going wrong with Joseph's and Martin's grades, Mr. Black made it better for them.

About that time, Josie was going to the same high school and had met the auto-mechanic teacher's nephew from a nearby town. Josie liked him, and Malcolm liked her; they planned to attend the same college.

One night, Malcolm was over; Mother had borrowed Mr. Black's car, and Malcolm recognized his uncle's car. Babe was silly and young and didn't know what discreet was. She joked about his uncle's car, but Malcolm didn't know that his uncle was having an affair since he knew that his uncle was married. Mr. Black lived in a rural town, and his wife didn't know anything either.

Mr. Black spent weekends at home with his wife, and sometimes, since he lived around the corner from the school,

Mother would spend evenings with him. Malcolm didn't live in town; he didn't know what was going on, and because Josie was blindly in love with Malcolm, she didn't think it mattered. It was the last year of high school for Josie, and she had made up her mind that she would join Malcolm in Miami, OK. It was the second year for Malcolm, and it would be the first year for Josie. Babe and Candi were glad to see Josie go to college and move away, and it wasn't long before JJ and Martin were on their own. JJ met a girl in the same apartment complex where Papa lived, and when she became pregnant, Mrs. Bird made him marry her, and then he had him a family. At least he graduated from school, both him and Martin. Martin ended up in Texas, away from everybody, but he had a good job, and he did well.

Staying in Aunt Etta's home was getting old because they never did any repairs, and after a while, the house began falling apart, but some new apartments in the neighborhood gave them hope that they would soon be moving into a bigger home, much bigger than the house they lived in, and it soon happened. By now, Babe and Candi were in high school, and they finally had their own bedroom, where Babe could talk and cry out to God whenever she wanted to. They had stopped going to church long ago since Mother didn't have a car, but nothing stopped Babe from going to her private space and talking to God.

One evening, when Babe was trying to understand the Bible, she kept reading about slaves and masters. Babe knew that her people had been slaves at one time, and she had heard some pretty bad things about it. She wondered if this was the way it should be since the Bible spoke of slaves as well. That evening, she cried out to God. "Please, God," she cried, "I know where Jesus came from and I believe in him but, God where, did you come from?" Babe cried with all her heart, and that evening, when she fell asleep, she awakened to a vision, a smoky cloud hanging over a big rock, and when she remembered it, she smiled; Babe knew that God was answering her, but she didn't know what it meant. From that point on, Babe decided to keep her spirituality within her heart to guard her innocence, yet she didn't want to deny her belief, so she just decided to wear a holy cross around her neck. Babe still enjoyed attending church, but with Mother not working, it seemed like they couldn't support anything in the church because she didn't have any money, and now Mother had turned to welfare completely. But they were all glad to have a bigger place with their own bedroom—nothing else mattered.

Now that Babe was in junior high school, all she could think of was getting a job. At thirteen years old, she would walk the neighborhood, going door-to-door at any business that was open, looking for a job. Her efforts finally paid off, but it was at school. One of the school counselors took Babe seriously and found her a job during lunchtime. However, after Babe left the kitchen, she would be soaking wet from washing dishes, making it difficult for her to return to class, but this problem was soon resolved after they switched her to a job after school, cleaning the teachers' lounge. Babe was paid every two weeks, and that check for $27 left her happy to be working. After giving her mom $9, it left her some money for school activities.

Babe was glad to be in school. She found her biology class to be one of the better classes, maybe because her teacher was so fond of her. Mrs. Alexander just loved Babe; she would let Babe help her after Babe finished cleaning out the teachers' lounge. Babe would help her take care of the pets in the classroom. At one point, Mrs. Alexander wanted Babe to take some papers home after school and grade them for her. Babe was looking forward to doing this, but after Mrs. Alexander talked it over with the school counselors, they didn't go along with it because it would make it too easy for Babe to know the answers without studying. But Babe did get to keep the hamsters one summer, along with a neighborhood friend. Glenda and Babe both got to keep a hamster one summer. This kept Mrs. Alexander from taking them home. Neither Babe nor Glenda had to buy a thing; she gave them the cage and all the food. All they had to do was feed the hamsters and clean the cage. Babe named her hamster Casper.

Babe's mom didn't care about having a hamster around; she said it looked like a rat or mice and boy did she scream loud when she found Casper running through the house. Babe knew what that meant. Casper had figured out how to get out of his cage, and every now and then, he would. Babe knew Casper got bored sometimes, so she started keeping Casper in her room where she could watch him better. Summer was about over, and it was time to return the hamsters back to school. Babe was glad that she took good care of her hamster, but Glenda's hamster didn't live through the summer, and they were sad about that. Mrs. Alexander knew she could count on Babe.

Babe had managed to find a job every summer through the government programs, and when she wasn't working on a summer job, she would find a few odd jobs in the neighborhood, babysitting and selling caramel apples and popcorn balls she had made. While selling caramel apples one day, she met a couple recruiting young kids for Bible school activities. The couple's name was Barb and Earnest, and they told Babe they were ambassadors for Christ through the Campus Crusade for Christ. They recruited kids from most north-side communities for fellowship. Campus Crusade for Christ visited the neighborhoods. Babe thought this was nice because some evenings were so boring, without enough to keep some of the kids out of trouble. Campus Crusade for Christ was a ministry for youths run by young adults. They would go to neighborhoods and witness to kids and offer them fun activities. They were planning a convention at the Camelot Hotel, and Barb and Earnest wanted to invite as many kids as they could. They even had boxes of peanuts to sell to pay for the registration.

Babe was excited about it; they even gave Babe a case of peanuts to sell for the convention. Babe, Glenda, and Candi went to the local shopping mall and stood outside selling the peanuts. Glenda happened to be a neighbor that lived a couple of doors down from the apartments.

It seemed like Babe and Glenda hit it off just fine. She was the only girl in her family also, but Glenda's brothers were nerve-racking. Clyde and Clark were smart when Babe first met them, but over the years, it seemed like the street drugs must have sizzled their brains because they became the geeks on the streets, and that wasn't in a smart way.

Finally, they had sold all the peanuts and were planning to attend the convention. The exciting thing about it was they were going to stay at the Camelot Hotel for an entire day and night—that was the best thing about it. Babe can't remember ever staying overnight anywhere and a hotel was the best place she could think of. Mother didn't mind, and they were off for the convention. It wasn't like they had to do much during summer, and this helped to fill the void in their poverty-stricken lives.

At the convention, it was all about finding yourself in the Lord. They made altar calls, and many young people committed to living for the Lord. Babe knew in her heart that she had made a commitment long ago, but she knew that she couldn't afford to take off and do the kind of work Barb and Earnest did because she needed a job. They were from a wealthy background, but Babe didn't care; she just knew that she had grown to love and respect them for all the love they had for God's people. After the convention, Barb and Ernest had lots of the kids from the projects over at their apartment where they had a pizza party. Barb said they did so well selling the peanuts they wanted to spend the money in a good way by treating the ones that helped sell them.

That summer was beautiful. Barb and Earnest went back to Carolina. Barb kept in touch with Babe. They eventually got married and had a child, but Babe lost contact with them. Babe knew it was God who put them in her life because as she grew in God and even though she realized she couldn't afford to attend college the way they did, she would still try to further her education while working until she was independent enough to help the way Earnest and Barb did.

Papa and Ms. Bird finally got married and officially became a couple. They didn't consider it a honeymoon, but Papa had a brother in Dayton, Ohio, who had been in the military, and Papa wanted to go visit his brother. He invited Candi and Babe to join them, along with Ester and the two of them.

Babe thought since Papa had a large-size car that could hit the road, in no time, they would be there. But the ride was long and weary, so Babe started taking her camera everywhere she went, and she was sure to make fun out of it.

Summer was upon them, and this ended up being a short vacation because after visiting Uncle Eddy, they had planned to visit the amusement park in Dallas, Texas. On the way back. However, Dayton, Ohio. Was a very long way from Tulsa, Oklahoma. They were in for a very long drive, and they had to stop every couple of hours at a rest stop.

When they got to Ohio, they met Uncle Eddy, who lived in a small home with his wife on the east side of town. Uncle Eddy was in bad health; he used an oxygen tank from time to time, and he walked with a cane. He didn't seem to be that old, about sixty-two, but the war had aged him faster.

Uncle Eddy had been married before, and he had two sons, Lonnie and Donnie, in Tulsa, but one moved to Chicago, Illinois, and the other one moved to Las Vegas, Nevada. Babe remembered Donnie being a smarty-pants. As a matter of fact, their mother used to life down the street from them in the new apartments that had just been built.

It was interesting to meet Papa's brother. There was only one still living in Tulsa, and then this one in Dayton, Ohio. Papa also had a sister living in Kansas City. The visit to Dayton was short but memorable. Uncle Eddy passed away several years after they visited him, but they were glad to have met him.

On the way back from Dayton, Ohio, it seemed faster until they stopped at the amusement park in Dallas, Texas. They had to walk so much it was tiring. They didn't have much money to spend, but it was the thought of Papa making an effort for everybody to be together that made Babe think of how nice it was.

After being divorced for five years, you'd think adults could get along better by now. Still Papa would stop by, and the senseless arguing would start. Mother didn't mind waking up the neighborhood.

As Babe grew up, Granny saw how ambitious Babe was, and she began to tell Babe to put her money away and try to save some of it every chance she got. Every summer, if she wasn't taking any summer-school classes, Babe would try to work. Babe had bought herself an old car by now, and she was going to do the right thing in life. Granny always thought Babe was a lot like her namesake; it seemed like Aunt Etta was outgoing, but since she didn't have as many children as Mother did, there was nothing to hold her back.

Living on government assistance allowed caseworkers to stop by periodically to make sure there wasn't a man living there, especially since Mother hadn't worked in years. But teenage pregnancy on the rise, there were also concerns of young girls becoming mothers before their time. Their visits were short and brief, but Mother would be well-informed of what they expected. After one of their meetings, Mother met with Candi and Babe and told them they would be going to see the doctor soon to get birth control pills.

Babe and Candi didn't know what to think because they had never been with a boy; they were still virgins. Mother never asked them anything; she just sent them to the doctor. The doctor prescribed them birth control pills to take. Now at fourteen and fifteen, the two young girls who did not even know about the birds and the bees were taking birth control pills, not even understanding how to take them. Before long, the pills messed up their cycle, and they're back at the doctor's office. The doctor couldn't believe their mother would put them on pills before she discussed it with them. He scorned their mother and told her that these girls didn't need any birth control pills.

While still at the doctor's office, Babe asked the doctor if she could have some diet pills. She had been plump all her life, and she didn't have a problem with boys because she figured she was too fat. The doctor smiled at her and told her to come back in a couple of more years if the diet plan, he gave her didn't work. Candi and Babe both were overweight, and because of that, they felt that the boys weren't interested in them.

Now that sex and birth control pills were behind her, Babe could concentrate on school and a job. Every summer, Babe and Candi would sign up for a summer job, and through the system, they usually ended up with one. They were glad to be able to make their own money. Candi got a job one summer at a different nursery, but it didn't last long. Candi didn't like school, and somehow, she and Babe were separated during senior high school. Candi had to go to school across town. Her grades were bad, and it was difficult for her to get along with people.

With the anticipation of senior year coming up, Babe wanted to look better; she wanted to drop those extra pounds she had been carrying for so long and, hopefully, start thinking about a boyfriend. Most of her classmates had boyfriends and were well on their way to going to college—at least, some of them. None of Babe's friends were mothers; they all graduated without the thought of changing diapers at the same time. A few talked about college, whereas others had to stay at home and work. It seemed like working was just as well, especially when it just wasn't financially possible to move away at the time.

Babe was sure about trying to lose weight, and after visiting the doctor again, it seemed like the pounds began to shed. She was fit for her graduation, and she tried to keep the weight off. However, after losing the pounds she had, Babe looked at her body and wondered what happened to her breast; it was baby fat like Papa said or it was the prayer she prayed. Nevertheless, Babe was glad to lose weight.

Now with all the festivities going on for high school seniors, Babe and a few friends were going to celebrate. Mary, one of Babe's friends who was Catholic, had gotten hold of some weed, and they were going to party in the town. Another friend had just broken up with her boyfriend, and she wanted to celebrate and find another boyfriend. But Babe thought, *why don't they find a good church and go to a revival?*

Mary was surprised that Babe was thinking about God at a time when they wanted to share their last year in school. Babe just wanted to play it safe, but she knew her friends were about as square as a box and nothing too bad could happen. Babe decided to let her guard down, and they all went out and partied and had such a good time. Mary passed the marijuana around, and they giggled, laughed, and had such a good time. Then they ate and grew tired and slept it off. Babe hadn't experienced marijuana, but it was fun for the occasion. Afterward, Babe was ready to regroup and put these things behind her and focus on the future.

Josie had been gone an entire year. She would write home from time to time. Babe liked having an older sister in college, trying to make a better life for herself, but it was a struggle for Josie; she didn't get any help financially from anybody, and when she would come home to visit, she would tell Babe how she had to shoplift sometimes. She had a job while in school, but it wasn't enough. The thought of going to college sounded great until she realized how hard it was for Josie. Josie resented Granny and how she helped Aunt Etta's children, Ammie and Don, while they went to college, but she couldn't help Josie as much. During Josie's first summer at home, it was discovered that she was pregnant, and they wanted to get married. At least Malcolm was a good man, and it seemed like he didn't mind doing the right thing.

Josie and Malcolm had a small reception in the apartments they lived at. Malcolm and Josie moved to Tulsa and made a home for their family, and soon little Markie was born, and Babe had a nephew to babysit. All was well—Malcolm got a good job with a grocery-store chain, and Josie tended to being a stay-at-home parent, and every now and then, she would pick up a job.

Babe and Candi were getting ready to graduate themselves. Babe had been working at an oil company since her last year in school, and she would continue to work there after school. Babe had planned on enrolling at the local junior college in Tulsa while working full time. Candi had an agenda of her own; she was busy looking for love. She didn't like school well enough to continue with it after graduation. She found a job at a hospital in housekeeping, and she liked it.

Both Babe and Candi graduated in the same year since Candi was held back when they were younger. It wasn't Candi's fault; they both struggled with school and getting good grades. Babe prayed and lucked out and charmed most of the people in her life; she didn't like to study. But to know that both looked forward to graduating and moving on, all Babe could think about was moving out on her own.

Now that all the children were grown, Mother had to think about doing something since government assistance would run out when all the children became eighteen years of age, and if they were not in college, she would be cut off from the program. Babe and Candi still gave Mom rent, but Babe knew she would eventually want her independence; she was an adult, and she wanted to live like an adult in her own place with her own rules, and not answering to anyone anymore.

Babe had worked most of her life already and she couldn't say anything about her mother's lifestyle, but she had hoped she could live a life according to the Bible and try to live the right way. James had been staying in California several years now, since Granny had brothers up there. James decided he would make his life with them, and every now and then, Granny would tell us that James wasn't doing so well; he would stay with other people and never had a place of his own.

Summer after graduation was just enough time to get involved with the crowds at the neighborhood park; it was always fun hanging out at the park, watching girls become ladies and boys become men. After graduating from school, Babe had bought herself a Chevy Vega, and it was fun to drive through the park, checking out the guys. The last guy she had eyes for was Erin, her softball coach. She met him while playing softball one year at the park. Erin was a couple of years older when they met, and Babe, being extremely shy when it came to boys, didn't know how to let him know how much she cared. She was reluctant because of her weight, and that's when Babe got serious about her diet, but now she didn't feel as self-conscious about being overweight. Babe and Glenda would circle the park; most of their friends wouldn't recognize Babe because she had lost about thirty pounds. She was glad to have all that weight off her.

That summer was hot, and the cars had filled up the parking lot. As Babe and Glenda waited for the traffic to move, Glenda noticed a brand-new Good Time van; it still had the new tag in the window. Glenda jumped for joy.

"Did you see him checking you out?" Glenda shouted.

"No, he wasn't," Babe responded. Babe kept on waiting for the traffic to move. As Babe looked up, it looked as if she caught a glance behind the smoke-tinted windows, but she couldn't be for sure. "Yes, probably," Babe said. *And How Many Other Women?* she thought.

Finally, they got a break and were able to leave the traffic behind. All Glenda could talk about was that red Good Times van. It was indeed nice, and any girl would enjoy a ride in it.

Babe decided the next time they saw it at the park, she would approach the driver and see if they could look inside just to strike up a conversation. After a couple of days, they were at the park again when the Good Time van parked right next to Babe. Glenda was with her, and she reminded Babe of what she said. Babe took a deep breath and stepped out of the car. As she approached the driver's side, he saw her coming and rolled his window down. Babe asked him if she and her friend could look at the inside of his van. He was nice to let them see. It was laidback, with a mini bar, a table, and a bed near the back window. They both complimented him for having nice taste. He asked Babe if she wanted to take a ride in it, and she said sure—of course, Glenda was right there with her.

After going several miles and back, they had an opportunity to learn about each other. By now he knew Babe's real name and she knew his. Howard lived in a neighborhood where Babe had grown up, and she knew of his family. He was about six years older than her. *But age was only a number after you reached legal age,* she thought. He asked her if he could call her sometime, and Babe was glad to give him her number. When he didn't call, she could only imagine that he must've thought she was too young.

Since Babe was in the process of looking for an apartment, she thought maybe when she would be on her own, she would not have a problem meeting a real man. Just as she was thinking that the phone rang. She answered, and it was Howard. He caught her off guard, but she was glad to hear from him. He invited her over to see his place later that evening, and he would pick her up. Babe wasn't going to pass up the chance to see him and know more about him.

Later that evening, Howard pulled up in the parking lot, and Babe didn't hesitate to dash out. The evening was early, so Howard suggested a movie since they still had the Motor Movie Drive-In, where they could stay in the van and watch the movie. The movie was an old Western one that neither one of them was into. They talked just so they had something to do while the movie played.

Howard told Babe that he had been in the marines and that he had a daughter. He claimed the mother had taken him to court over the paternity of the child. Babe listened intently as she thought he didn't need any more children, at least anytime soon.

They went to Howard's apartment and talked over a glass of wine and eventually found themselves wrapped in each other's arms. Howard began to move his hand over Babe's body, and before she knew anything, his hands were removing her clothes and she had to pull back.

"I'm not ready," she said.

He was upset, but Babe insisted she was ready to go home. As she prepared to leave, she thanked him for the night out.

On the way home, everything was quiet, and Babe could tell that he was giving her the silent treatment. Babe was proud that she didn't get pregnant during school, but she still didn't want to risk that chance now either. When Howard pulled up to Babe's apartment complex, he asked her if they could see each other later, and she agreed. Babe was a little baffled that he didn't seem concerned about protection, yet she began to think about what kind of protection she could get since she wanted to be with him. It seemed like the normal thing to do; everyone was doing it, so that gave her the seal of approval. Babe wondered if the birth control pills were still at work for her. Foolishly, Babe thought that it would be great, but being unsure, she decided to check with others. They also had foam that she could buy over the counter.

Howard did call again to see if Babe wanted to go fishing with him. He drove up this time with a boat on the back of his van. Babe was all set to go fishing, and it was a nice weekend for fishing. The fish were biting, and as the evening approached, they decided to get back before the sun went down. Back at Howard's apartment, he cleaned the fish and cooked some for dinner. After they ate, he asked Babe if she wanted to spend the night.

"Only if I don't have to sleep with you."

"Not again," he said. "I thought you're going to get protection."

She told him she's still looking for the best kind. Then she asked him what he had. He pulled out a pack of condoms and said that they worked all the time.

"Hum!" Babe sighed, "I would rather wait."

After cleaning the kitchen together, they relaxed in front of the television and cuddled against each other. The warmth of their bodies only led to more touching and kissing, and before she could say anything, he was inside of her. She couldn't resist him any longer; she knew that she wanted him as well. Morning was near, and they were still at it, and Babe wondered how it happened so fast.

Howard smiled at her and said, "Sometimes you can't fight nature."

Babe couldn't deny it was wonderful, but she had a concern and a worry as well; she couldn't remember Howard slipping on the condom. Babe ended up spending the entire weekend with Howard, and it was carefree until she got home and started feeling guilty and thinking how irresponsible she was. She prayed to God that nothing would go wrong. Howard dropped her off Sunday night because she had to work that Monday.

At work on Monday, Babe couldn't stop thinking about what a good time she had with Howard, but she feared it would cost her the unimaginable. She tried to stay busy to keep from thinking about him, but when she didn't hear from him that week, Babe began to think he had dumped her. It wasn't like they had known each other that long. Something just happened. Babe left a message on his phone, but he hadn't returned her calls. Babe had still been looking for an apartment, and the one she had left a deposit on called her and told her the apartment was ready. Since the apartment was ready, Babe figured she would just move; he'd come around.

The apartments on Seventh Street weren't far from her mom's place, and since she didn't have much to move in, she figured she would buy things later after she got settled in. Babe hadn't heard from Howard yet, and after work, she would rush over to Mother's just in case he called. Babe didn't have a phone in her new apartment yet, so she would drag out staying over at Mother's place until it was late before going to her apartment. Every now and then, Babe would pass by the park to see if she would see Howard. Babe's hurt turned into upset when she realized that she had missed her period. She double-checked the dates and thought she could be pregnant. *Dear God,* she prayed, *don't let this be.*

The next morning, she woke to nausea and vomiting, and the thought upset her more. Babe let another week go by before getting checked. She didn't want to deal with the problem yet, but as soon as the test proved that she was pregnant, she had already reasoned with herself that the relationship wasn't right; they both had been driven by their lustful desires, and now she had a bigger problem on her hands.

Babe knew Howard was under no obligation to marry her. Alone in her apartment, she cried, "God, I've made a terrible mistake, but does that mean I have to live with It?"

Babe knew that she eventually wanted a child but not any kind of way; she wanted a husband, and she didn't want one without the other. As the sorrow deepened, the gut feeling of being another welfare recipient wouldn't leave. Babe realized how their home wasn't much of a home after her father left and how it would be unfair to bring a child into a world without a responsible father, especially after coming from a broken family herself. Babe just didn't want that kind of struggle. First and foremost, Babe realized that she had sinned, and she alone would need to repent of that. Babe admitting to error in sin was the key to solving the problem and moving on would open her eyes to growing up.

There was no way Babe could afford to raise a child, and she couldn't imagine depending on government assistance and staying with her mother to raise the child. Abortion was the best way out as she thought about something Howard said about his daughter. That's when Babe realized that he was not ready for any more children. Babe knew she didn't want to go through that without a man.

Babe made an appointment to talk with a counselor at an abortion clinic, but she cried so much they had to reschedule her. Again, she tried to contact Howard without any success. *This is senseless,* Babe thought. She knew what to do and informing him shouldn't make any difference. It would make it more difficult, she thought. Her second appointment was a charm; the fetus was terminated, and Babe wanted to know if they had a procedure to use to keep this from ever happening again. The doctor told her to go with the instructions they gave her and return in a month. They had a device that would be a permanent fixture to use as birth control. After the doctor's visit, Babe was thankful that she hadn't told Howard so she could move on.

At work, a friend knew Howard and told Babe that her sister-in-law was also pregnant by Howard, and another lady as well. When Babe found this out, she felt relieved that she didn't go through with the pregnancy. The decision to have the abortion created a financial setback since Babe had moved into an apartment. She decided to move back home with Mother until it was the right time to move again.

Babe knew never to say a word to her mother about the abortion because she didn't want her to know. But somehow Candi knew about it because she had been dating the love of her life, and he wanted Candi to have his children, and Candi wanted to have his children because she loved Stefan.

Candi and Stefan had been dating for over two years, and when Candi knew that she was pregnant, she was so happy because she knew this was what Stefan wanted. When Babe told Candi what she had done, Candi was upset with Babe because if Babe had carried her fetus to term, they would have both had children around the same age, but Babe didn't care about any of that.

Babe knew that Howard was too unpredictable to be another father, but Candi and Stefan had a stable relationship. At least it seemed like it, but the closer the time for Candi to have her baby, the more Candi couldn't count on him. Babe was glad that Candi was happy to be having a baby, but when she was in labor for over thirty hours, Babe thought, *and to think I would be doing the same for a father that wouldn't even be there.*

Babe had bought all kinds of gifts for Candi's baby, and somehow, they knew it was going to be a girl. Babe even had to take Candi to the hospital because they couldn't find Stefan at the time, but the last and final time Candi went to the hospital, Stefan never did show up, even when the baby was born. Babe couldn't believe it. She thought, *they had planned this child together, and now, Stefan didn't even show up to put his name on the birth certificate.* Babe tried to understand since Stefan came from a big family and his father never did marry his mother because he was already married. His father's first wife just wanted one child, but his father wanted as many as he could have—that's how Stefan ended up with so many half-brothers and sister.

But within his immediate family, there were at least eight siblings. It still seemed hard to grasp because this was his first child. Candi and Stefan weren't married, but Babe understood that's the way life was. Eventually Stefan and Candi married and Stefan proved he could be a responsible father.

When Stefan didn't show up at the hospital even to sign the birth certificate, Babe thought, *So Much for Stability.* Babe had moved back home with her mother for now; however, she didn't want to stay too long.

Josie and Malcolm had settled in and were glad to be in Tulsa. Josie knew that Malcolm missed his family; they were close, and after Malcolm managed to get a house, it wasn't long before Malcolm was moving his family to Tulsa as they had all lived in Shawnee, Oklahoma. Josie was fine with that.

After the entire family got settled in, Josie joined them in their religion, Jehovah's Witness. Mother's dear friend Paula—whom Josie stayed with after their parents' divorce since the house was too small for six children—used to be a Jehovah's Witness. Babe had attended church with Paula at times, and she thought it was different, but then, most are. They didn't make a big deal about giving either. Now here, Josie was going door-to-door witnessing. Josie started trying to witness to people. Babe didn't want to be rude, but she lifted her cross from around her neck and told Josie, "Jesus is the only one for me."

There was something about the witnesses that made Babe think that they didn't believe in Jesus—she really didn't know. Before long, Josie was trying to match Babe with Malcolm's brother. Babe thought that it was just too close for comfort. They're both nice-looking men, but Babe couldn't believe that Josie could date him after knowing that their mother and their married uncle were kicking it, or however you would say it.

Babe never told Josie about the abortion; she figured she might not be able to stomach it, but Josie knew that Babe had moved back home with Candi and Mother, and Candi told her.

Josie suggested to Babe that she apply for a HUD home, like the one they lived in. She knew Babe had pretty good credit since she had been working before high school and had established a long line of credit. Babe thought about what Josie had said and thought she would investigate it. When Babe found out that she could own a three-bedroom house with a yard and a fence, she decided that it would be great. She found a house out north, and she applied for it with no problems; her exceptional credit approved her application. Babe prepared to move again, but this time, she hoped that it was for good.

Chapter 2

Moving On

Moving into a three-bedroom house at 4120 N. Franklin Avenue was a blessing. The house was government-owned and had to meet inspections, which granted its good condition since it had no appliance or air-conditioning. It looked as though Babe would be holding down a second job for quite some time.

Glenda helped Babe move in, and with the few items she owned, it didn't take long. After a couple of loads, everything was unpacked and neatly put in its proper place. When they came back with the last load, Glenda noticed a friend of hers living at the corner house. When she invited him over, Babe felt apprehensive since they both began to smoke marijuana. Marijuana usually made Babe cough; luckily, she never acquired a habit for it. Glenda and Babe had planned to spend the evening at the shopping mall where a musical festival was scheduled, so they cut the conversation short. Glenda's friend refused their invitation to go along.

Babe returning home alone was a bad discovery—she had been burglarized. The backroom window was still open, indicating a way of entrance. Alone, Babe paced through the house, trying to fight the fear building within her. The few valuables she owned were stolen. Babe pictured Glenda's friend in her mind. She called the police, and soon officers were on the scene, investigating the backyard and the house. One officer wrote the report as they talked. Babe mentioned to him that she suspected Glenda's friend. Both officers were sympathetic when they learned she had just moved in that very day. Reporting the loss to the insurance company first thing Monday morning was the biggest disappointment because, unfortunately, the deductible was more than her loss, and for consequential reason, they advised her not to submit a claim.

Babe's grief over the loss was accepted after reasoning with herself that it could have been worse. She began to thank God that she didn't have much that could have been stolen. After that incident, Babe made sure she checked all the windows and tried to secure them down better with a nail through the middle of the window to prevent it from opening too easily.

Glenda and Babe kept in touch, and when Glenda found out Babe had been burglarized that same night they went to the festival, Glenda agreed with Babe that the burglar was the guy she had invited over. Glenda apologized to Babe since she was the one who invited him over. Babe figured she didn't know that he would come back to rob her. Glenda told Babe that they ought to go out and put the whole thing behind them. Babe thought that would do her fine.

That evening, they headed out to the Full-Moon Nightclub. At the club, Glenda and Babe partied awhile, but when Babe looked up, to her surprise, she saw Howard. Babe didn't know what to do. She knew if they talked, she would end up telling him about the abortion, so she tried to avoid him. It was all too obvious after he saw her that they would talk.

Howard asked Babe for a dance, and after dancing to a few songs, they sat down and talked. She told Howard how she tried to reach him after they had spent that romantic weekend together, but she failed to contact him.

Now Babe had moved to another place altogether. Howard wanted to keep in touch with Babe; she thought that, at least, it would give her a chance to tell him what she did. Babe hadn't told Glenda about the abortion, so upon leaving the club, when Glenda joked with Babe about lighting the flame with Howard, Babe said that she doubted that very seriously; it was then that Babe decided to tell Glenda about the abortion. Babe told Glenda about the other women that Howard had impregnated and how she would've been the third one if she hadn't gotten an abortion.

Glenda's expression froze when Babe told her. "You didn't," Glenda said, but Babe assured her.

Babe went on to tell Glenda about a paternity suit Howard was already going through. Then Glenda told Babe that the baby was a part of her.

"A part of me that made a mistake," Babe said.

Glenda was the only girl in her family; Babe couldn't help but wonder if that's why she felt the way she did. Glenda expressed her disappointment in Babe, but Babe couldn't let Glenda get the best of her. Glenda couldn't figure out why Babe would still be interested in talking with Howard since the flames had burned out for him. Babe just told her that she wanted to put some closure on the matter.

Later that week, Howard did call Babe, and they got together. When they had time to talk together, Babe told Howard about the pregnancy and the abortion. He seemed upset and told her that she had no right to do that. Babe argued that she tried to contact him, but to no avail. Babe couldn't cry about it because she was strong now, and when he realized how well she was dealing with it, he promised her he would give her another baby. Babe just listened to him, thinking that he must be crazy. She didn't feel that she was no better off than when it first happened. Now you would think that he would realize how he would take care of all the children he already had, but Babe never told him that she knew about the others.

Babe wondered after that if that's all some men wanted to do. Babe avoided Howard after that; she knew it was some sort of game to him. He would call her all the time, wanting to get together, but Babe knew it would never happen again. Babe was anxious to look for an extra job after that. She knew if she were busy, she wouldn't think about him or having a boyfriend. She thought she could take one course at the junior college and work an extra job to get the things she needed.

After applying for a job at the department store, it didn't take long to see that part of her salary was going to purchases, but she decided to stay there anyway for a couple of months. The department-store job was nice, but Babe found too many things to buy with her check.

A local hospital was hiring evening janitorial work. It wasn't far from her home, so Babe decided to switch jobs; that way, she wouldn't be tempted to buy things in the store. After switching the part-time job, it looked like the class at the junior college had to take a backseat. Switching over to the other job gave Babe the weekends off.

Josie only stayed about six miles from Babe. She would visit regularly, and Josie would transport and run errands for Mother since Mother didn't have a car. Mother depended on her kids to help her when they could. Since Josie didn't have to work, she transported Mother to the store and doctor and wherever else she needed to go. One evening, Josie stopped by; she told Babe to expect a phone call from James, their brother in California.

Phone Call from James, Babe wondered, whatever for?

Later that evening, while Babe was trying to clean, the phone rang. "Hello, Babe" the voice on the other end spoke; Babe recognized James's voice right off.

"What a surprise—then again, not exactly. Josie told me you would be calling."

James congratulated Babe on her new home, and then he proceeded to tell her about a friend of his that wanted to attend Spartan School of Aeronautics and would need a place to stay. Remembering the burglary, Babe thought that it would be a good idea. She had completely furnished her home with used furniture, and she was roommate ready.

Hank arrived at the airport within a week; he stood about five feet nine, a lightweight man who looked to be about thirty. He recognized Babe right off. James must've described her or showed him a picture of her.

It was mid-January, and Hank was shivering in a thin sports jacket.

"What's the temperature?" he wanted to know.

"About twenty degrees," Babe answered.

"Back in California, people were wearing shorts," he explained.

The two suitcases he carried didn't seem like an awful lot since his stay was to be a couple of years before his studies were completed. As soon as they got home, he unpacked and lit up a stick of marijuana. His weed-smoking left Babe concerned. Hank had $500 in cash to help him with necessities. He offered Babe some money for his stay, but she refused. She explained to him that she would allow him to stay three months, all expenses paid, then after that, she would charge him $90 a month to cover bills and food if he decided to stay on. He said that it seemed fair enough, and he agreed.

Hank noticed Babe's crucifix, which hung about her neck, and he quickly proclaimed that he was Buddhist and didn't believe in God.

"To each his own," Babe said and turned away.

Hank wanted a response from Babe, so he continued exalting his beliefs. Babe didn't like to get into conversations about religion; she felt it was a personal matter, especially since she didn't attend church or follow the traditional Christian way—meaning, she was still a sinner saved by grace.

Babe felt she wasn't qualified to explain. Hank was determined to know why she believed in God. Finally, Babe told him, "I know that I believe that God is real. He's almighty over any other god. And it's really not important to know anymore."

Afterward, Babe felt like an idiot and began to think of how silly she must be to wear a cross and not be able to explain her belief to others. Then she remembered reading in the Bible, "The secret things belong to the Lord." Besides, she felt there were enough preachers in the world without her help; furthermore, everyone was always talking about how complicated it seems to understand the Bible, so Babe grew content in just believing.

When friends came to visit Babe, she would introduce them to her new roommate, and he would quickly leave to go to his room to chant. They all thought he was strange, and Babe became embarrassed by his actions. As they would talk in the living room, Hank would start his chanting, which would get louder and louder. Babe had to turn the stereo up sometimes. This would drown out the chanting, but it never worked. Behind his back, they joked about him.

The weather remained cold, and Hank was forced to purchase a coat, boots, and thermal wear. Soon he found a job, and they carpooled to work. Babe noticed how irresponsible he acted. Rather than writing to his family, he made long-distance phone calls instead. Babe and Hank began to argue. They argued about the smallest things. One of the biggest problems was shunning off his flirtatious remarks.

Three months had passed, and Hank met new friends at school, some of whom came to the house to visit. Two of these friends, John and Tony, became very fond of Babe, which, in turn, brought out a side of Hank Babe hadn't seen before. She began to show interest in Tony because Hank was beginning to grate her nerves. She decided to date Tony because she thought he was nice looking, and she wanted Hank to know she wasn't interested in him.

Eventually, Babe could see that their platonic friendship wasn't getting any better. They disagreed on too many things. His chanting to his Buddha was driving away the peace Babe once enjoyed in her home. The phone bill continued to mount because of his out-of-town phone calls. Babe felt it was best that he moved out, and because he didn't know anyone in Tulsa, Babe was relieved when he decided to move in with his friends. Tony and Babe didn't date long since Hank got the message, and Babe realized she really wasn't interested in Tony. It took Hank six months to pay back the phone bills and rent, and they did become better friends after he left. Now Babe's friends came to visit more often.

One evening, Pam a friend stopped by to tell Babe about her part-time job at a club, and she asked if Babe would be interested in working with her. Babe didn't see how she could fit it in with her two other jobs; Pam explained the hours were 10:00 pm until

2:00 am. Since her other part-time job ended at 9:00 pm, Babe began to seriously consider her offer.

Babe asked, "When can I start."

Pam answered, "This weekend."

The first weekend at the club was more like a party than a job. Serving drinks and meeting the customers seemed to put zeal back into Babe's social life. After working at the club for about a month, the tips and paycheck allowed her to quit her second job at the hospital. The club was more interesting than the hospital, and the hours allowed Babe her evenings back. Working at the club was more like entertainment than work. Babe met many new people and received tips on the best after-parties.

A girl named Brenda came to work at the club. When she found out Babe had a three-bedroom house, she asked if she could be her roommate. After thinking it over, Babe agreed, especially since Brenda would be leaving for college at the end of summer.

With Brenda living with Babe, there were always plenty of guests stopping by. One evening, a host of friends came by, and they all gathered in the den, watching television and talking. After the movie ended, they showed the guests out, then they both prepared for bed in their separate rooms. When she was in her bedroom, a strange feeling came over Babe. She looked around to try to figure out what it was. Then she noticed her bedroom window, which she kept open for fresh air. The screen had been unlocked.

Her suspicions were confirmed when Babe couldn't find her purse the next morning, before leaving for work. Babe had reached for her purse, but it wasn't there. Frantically, she searched her mind for the last place she had put it, and she knew it had been in her bedroom. Had someone entered her bedroom while they entertained in the opposite room? Although Babe still wasn't sure the purse had been stolen, she called the police and gave them full details for their files. They said they would let her know if they found anything. After they left, Babe went to work, wondering all the while who would be brash enough to enter her house while they entertained guests.

A week passed before the police contacted Babe. They had located the purse. It was found in a creek about a mile from her home. Babe was surprised to get the purse back although everything inside was missing. Babe was glad that all she had in it was $10. After that experience, Babe hated to see Brenda leave. Brenda was planning to leave in two weeks if she could manage to get fifty dollars for her registration. The deadline date was close to her enrollment. She came to Babe in need of a loan, and realizing how important it was to her, Babe rearranged her budget and loaned it to her. Brenda would be leaving, but the incident of the stolen purse had Babe thinking about installing bars on her windows. The salesman also sold her a door-attachment alarm. The bars were installed not long after Brenda moved. Babe hoped it would prevent any more thefts. The alarm system turned out to be a contraption that was quite time consuming.

Soon Babe had another roommate who needed a place to stay until she could afford her own apartment. An old classmate introduced Babe to Sandi. She loved to party occasionally. Sandi met one of JJ's friends even though he was married, and she took up with him. Sandi and Gary had planned on joining Babe at the club one night where she worked. Gary left early, and after the club closed, Babe and Sandi went home, laughing about the good time Gary and Sandi had while Babe worked the night away. At the house, Babe attempted to unlock the front door, but it alarmed her to see the door was already unlocked.

"Something's wrong," Babe said.

They stepped inside to see a ramshackle mess. Babe held her purse in front of her as though it was a stick to use.

"Let's get out of here while we can," Sandi insisted.

As Babe called the police, she tried to calm Sandi down by telling her. "Whoever did this is long gone."

The police arrived and discovered the bar on the back of the window had been pried off and left on the ground. The burglar had entered the window and left out the front door.

Some Security System, Babe thought.

Sandi was pretty upset because some of her things were damaged as well, and she didn't have insurance. Babe agreed to give her a portion of the claim she received. The claim was smaller than she expected after the depreciation was figured, which didn't allow much for either one of them. She agreed to adjust Sandi's rent to make up the difference, but Sandi wasn't satisfied with her portion, so she moved out. Later, Babe felt bad about the disagreement, but she began to think something suspicious about Gary and suspected her roommate, since she was dating a married man, and it could've been a setup.

It was nice having her privacy again. Those pleasant moments had been missed. Babe had a weekend off at the club and was excited about the free time. As she mowed and picked up the yard, a neighborhood boy stopped by. They visited for about an hour before Babe realized how late it was. She told him that she was going out that night because this was her first weekend off in a long time. He left, and Babe went inside and fixed herself a cocktail to help her unwind. An attempt to call a friend to join her was made, but no one was home; a second friend was called, a college classmate who had recently made a conversion in faith. When Mary began to witness to Babe, Babe told her she knew all about that; Babe said she wasn't ready to make a commitment that she couldn't live up to.

Mary reminded Babe that during senior high school, all Babe talked about was going to a revival, and now she's blending in with the world. Babe reminded Mary, "We are in the world then, are we not?"

Mary thought for a minute and agreed; she then told Babe to be careful and that she would pray for her.

Babe told Mary, "I still talk to God, but I like to party, and I don't see anything wrong with it. I thank God even when I'm dancing."

After hanging up, Babe thought about what Mary said, and she considered her lifestyle. Babe was afraid if she went to church, she would lose her joy, with nothing to look forward to. Babe was glad when Mary said she would pray for her.

Babe changed into a party dress, but the cocktail she had fixed herself was beginning to take its toll. She relaxed her head because it felt heavy. A good night's sleep was what she needed instead. At that moment, the doorbell rang.

There stood Troy, a friend whom she didn't want to be bothered with. She told him she was on her way to Disco World nightclub just to get rid of him for that moment. Troy suggested that he meet her there. After he left, Babe lay across her bed fully dressed, and the doorbell rang one more time.

Curious, she looked out the window, and this time, it was a friend named Bob, a guy from her day job. Babe didn't go to the door. Men friends were never rare but being able to trust them proved difficult.

By now, Babe had changed her mind about going out, and her neighbor's dog was the only thing that was preventing her sleep. This dog seemed to bark at everything. When the fence began to rattle, Babe simply turned over in bed, thanking God for his love before she fell asleep.

Subconsciously, Babe thought she had heard a loud thump. Totally stiffed out, she figured it was a picture frame from the wall, so she ignored the commotion.

The next day, Babe woke up early. She thought to check out the noise she heard the night before, which she assumed was a picture that had fallen. After using the bathroom, Babe went to the living room to see what had fallen. She didn't see anything in the living room or on the floor; she decided to see if the kitchen was intact. When Babe stepped in the kitchen, to her dismay, the door had been kicked in. She held herself tight and thought, *someone had come in the house last night while I was fast asleep.* She Thanked God and knew his angels were watching over her. All that noise she heard, she was glad she didn't get up to check it out, or she would have faced the person head-on, and that might not have been too good.

The next day was Sunday, and if there was any reason to go to church, it would have been that day, but Babe had praised God at home while she was working on getting the door fixed. She couldn't imagine who, for the life of her, could have done this. She thought about the two visitors she had before she fell deep into sleep, but she didn't think it could've been Troy. She knew he was bold, but he didn't have any reason to be, then she thought of Bob, whom she didn't even answer the door for, but neither one was that way at all.

While she was in the garage, she opened the garage door and a car drove by slowly. It was the young neighbor she had talked with yesterday, who was a good kid, but the way he slowed down as he drove by made Babe think of that kid; and all along Babe thought he was nice. A few of the neighbors' houses had been broken in, and they would tell Babe a thing about the neighborhood.

Across the street were good neighbors and next door as well, but this kid lived at the end of the block, and Babe really didn't know him. She didn't mind being nice to people, but she didn't realize that she should not tell people her business. Then she recalled how she told the kid she was going out that night, and he thought she had gone out. Babe thought how stupid it was for her to hold a conversation with strangers and tell them anything. *When will I learn?* she thought. One of her neighbors told her that not only was the neighborhood full of thugs and thieves, but also a mile away, there were bad kids that looked for houses to target.

Babe started thinking she liked living in her house, and she didn't want to move, but she didn't want to entice anyone or make herself a target, and she didn't want to be rude to people either.

Babe had been working at the nightclub for a while now; she enjoyed meeting different people. One night at work, she was busy trying to take orders when, suddenly, a young man at a table all by himself stopped her and asked her to take his order. He wanted a Coke. She brought back his Coke, and he introduced himself to her.

"The name is Patrick Dell," he said in a deep voice. "Have you ever done modeling?"

Babe thought about her high-school pictures and said, "'Sure," hoping he would never ask to see them. She had lost some weight now, and she wasn't as fat. "Mr. Dell—," Babe said.

He interrupted, "Call me Patrick."

Jokingly Babe said, "Of course, you don't look any older than me."

Patrick reached out and gave her a card. He told her to call him; he would like for her to join a group that would be modeling at the Performing Arts Theater. Babe thought, *why not? That Would Make Life Interesting. Who knows? A better job than waiting tables could be in the making.*

Later, when things slowed down a bit, Babe pulled the card out and looked at it. "Devonte Modeling Agency Patrick Dell".

Babe figured he didn't look like a big businessman, but no one should despise small beginnings. She figured she would call him later and see what's up with it.

That week, Babe had enrolled in a real-estate class and was looking forward to doing something in real estate on the side. Monday night was class night, and it wasn't until late when she got out of class. After Babe got home, she reached over to hang her keys up and saw Patrick's card. She wondered if it was too late to call him. At 9:00 pm, she figured she would dial his number and see what happened.

As the phone rang, Babe wondered what to expect.

"Hello," a voice answered.

"Is Patrick there?" Babe asked.

The voice responded, "One moment." "Patty!" someone shouted in the background.

"Hello," another voice answered.

Babe asked, "Is this Patrick?"

He responded, "Yes, it is, who is asking?"

"Hi, we met in the club the other night. They call me Babe, but my real name is Valleta Juanetta Johnson."

"I'm glad you called. Babe, can we meet at the park tomorrow for a photo shoot?"

Babe thought, *That's Sudden.* " But when she realized her, next class would be the day after she said, "Better now than Wednesday."

"What's happening on Wednesday?" he asked.

"I'm taking classes three nights a week, which are Mondays, Wednesdays, and Fridays."

"Well, tomorrow it is."

"Which Park?" Babe asked.

"O'Brien Community Park, out north."

After getting all the details, it was agreed that they would meet there at 5:00 pm the next day.

At work the next day, Babe daydreamed about the photo shoot. He had told her to wear something comfortable. She didn't think much about Patrick. For some reason, modeling sounds more fun than getting to know him. After work that evening, she went home and changed first and then met Patrick at the park. Babe could tell Patrick wasn't a big-time photographer because he had a little instant camera, but when they began to share about each other, they both found out they were first cousins.

They were a hit as they talked about their families and Babe found out that Uncle Will, Babe's papa's brother, had a kid out of wedlock, and it was still a secret. Babe felt badly for Patrick since Uncle Will was still in denial. Uncle Will was married at the time, and his first wife left him and moved to Michigan. Babe wondered if she knew about Patrick. After finding out that they were related, Babe and Patrick became good friends. They rehearsed up until the fashion show.

Sometimes they would meet at the other park with the other girls that would be modeling, and they would all rehearse together. Babe's schedule became too busy to work at the club on the weekends, so she decided, with the classes she was taking and preparing for the modeling show, she had to drop the nightclub job. She didn't mind because she had paid off enough bills, and she thought the show would be fun.

When Babe found out it was for charity, she forgot about getting paid. Meeting Patrick's family was interesting; he had older brothers Babe had already met while working in the club. His brothers were all nice looking, and Patrick wasn't bad looking himself. Patrick's mother had died, but he stayed with his auntie. Patrick's brothers were the kind that was always in trouble. Babe remembered meeting Troy and Gary before she had met Patrick; they didn't have the same father, so they weren't related to Babe like Patrick.

Babe and her papa kept in touch. One weekend, she decided to pay him a visit and inform him about the upcoming fashion show. Babe knew that Papa worked out of his cousin's garage. When Babe got there, there were still a few people getting their cars serviced. Babe mentioned to Papa that she met Uncle Will's son Patrick, but Papa didn't remember him.

Anyway, Babe proceeded to tell Papa about the fashion show she would be modeling in, and she told him she would find out about the tickets since Patrick was taking care of all of that. Babe left thinking he acted as if he didn't know Patrick. Babe could tell it seemed like Patrick despised his father for not accepting him.

Babe knew Uncle Will's first wife and daughter; Josie and his daughter were about the same age, and they played together when they were younger. Jonni was her name, and she was the only child Uncle Will had, and now to hear about Patrick. Babe had heard that Uncle Will had remarried after his first wife left him and went to Michigan, but he didn't have any children by his second wife.

As Babe was unlocking the front door, she heard the phone ringing. She reached it just in time.

"Hello?" Patrick was on the other end. "I was just thinking about you," Babe said.

"You were?"

"Yes, I was wondering about the tickets, who's selling them, and where a person can buy them if they want to attend." Babe mentioned to Patrick that she saw her father and told him about Patrick. Patrick told her he didn't remember him.

Patrick said he was quite young when he saw her papa, and his mother was still living at the time. That's how he met his daddy; his mom took him over to see his father's family. Patrick did look like Uncle Will—he had his height and facial features. If they had DNA testing during that time, it would probably be a match, and now that time has passed, most people just let bygones be bygones.

As they switched the conversation back to the show, Patrick told Babe that if she wanted to give a few tickets to the family, he would get some for her. Everything happened so fast Babe didn't know if she had told anyone else in the family. Everyone was scattered, and she didn't actually think it was going to happen. Candi was on her own now; she had a family and a husband, and it was seldom that they ever saw each other. It was then that Babe thought they were probably not interested in attending anyway.

During the last rehearsal at the park, Patrick told Babe to be ready to be fitted. That night, Babe was fitted for two really cute outfits: One was a two-piece—a beige after-five strapless jumpsuit with knickerbockers made from sheer, soft chiffon fabric. It included a throw around for her shoulders. The other was a casual two-piece—a red, black, and white plaid skirt and white blouse, which was fitting for a day at the office.

After trying them both on and strutting around the room as they practiced, Babe felt like a million dollars. She knew that they were much too expensive for her to own, but she was glad to have a chance at modeling them. They had to label the outfits for the fashion show after taking them off. Her name was pinned on the top, so now she knew what she would be wearing. She would have to match up her own shoes.

Babe knew just the pair—her two-inch heels would be perfect, with their thin straps and open toes. She wore them every now and then at the club. Patrick seemed to know all the other girls as well. Babe didn't know any of them; she didn't have time when they were at rehearsal. She figured, with her classes and all, she did well to squeeze the fashion show in.

Plans were being made for the fashion show that weekend, and Babe had asked Papa if he could come, but he had other things planned. Patrick informed Babe they would be taking pictures, so she thought maybe she could buy the pictures and prove that she was actually in a fashion show.

Everyone participating in the show had gathered in the back, behind the stage. With all the chattering going on, no one was aware of the audience waiting behind the curtain. The director gave his pep talk and encouraged everyone to do their best, and Babe modeled her first outfit: the casual plaid—a red, black, and plaid skirt. While she waited for her cue, she began to be somewhat nervous. Babe had rehearsed quite a bit, and she didn't think she would freeze, but when she saw the crowd behind the curtains, she was glad that all she had to do was walk down the runway, turn, and come back.

But not so fast, she thought.

She calmed herself as she heard her number, which meant it was her turn. Gallantly, she walked to the beat of the music as she held her head high, looking to see if she recognized anyone, but she didn't.

Babe thought: "If only family could see me now"

The flashing of camera lights startled her for a minute, but she gained her composure, turned, and returned behind the curtains. Others cheered her as they all prepared to exit on schedule.

Quickly Babe headed for the dressing room to change into the other outfit, the one that she felt was erotically dashing. Babe thought this one was the best. She wished she could use it on a night out, for she knew she would turn heads with it.

As she rushed to model her second outfit, the program was almost over, and she was glad she had saved the best for last. Patiently she waited until her number sounded again.

Confidently she strutted like a peacock, holding her head back as she tossed the wrap around her shoulder to reveal her bare shoulders, then she positioned the wrap around her waistline and then around her neck. As she approached the end of the runway, Babe turned and headed back toward the curtain. She almost lost her footing when the heel of her shoe bent over. Babe hoped it wasn't noticeable when she skipped a beat, but then got right back on track.

Wow! That Was Close, she thought.

After the show, Patrick invited Babe to join him and some friends for drinks at the club in the hotel next to the Performing Arts Theater. They had live entertainment as they socialized, and they ate peanuts and popcorn. It was getting late, and Babe knew she still had more studying to do—a couple more chapters and she would be finished with the real estate course and preparing for the exam would be next.

Chapter 3

Bewildered Yet Beloved

The modeling days were behind Babe, and there wasn't going to be anymore that she knew of. Patrick had made himself an agent for the occasion. Babe and Patrick agreed to keep in touch; they were like family now. And the thought of how Babe met Patrick opened her eyes to a whole new world. Babe realized that she was blessed to have met him even if it was in a club.

The pictures were ready, and Babe needed to go pick out the ones she wanted. When Babe saw the pictures, she thought, *Look at me! Wow!* She looked like a real model. Who would have known she was just doing it for the fun of it? Babe had another week, and she was going to go to Oklahoma City for the real estate exam. She found herself studying all night long, and sometimes, she would close herself in and just study.

After work one evening, Babe closed herself in her bedroom and didn't come out. She studied all night long. She had forgotten to turn the porch light on, and suddenly, Babe woke to some noise, and as she turned to check on it, a dark shadowy figure ran toward her. Before she knew anything, he was upon her with a knife at her throat.

Babe shocked at what was happening just followed the man's demands. He ordered her to the hallway where he stripped her of her clothing and assaulted her. He covered her face with a pillowcase and ordered her to stay there until he left. As Babe listened for him to leave, she thought, *Dear God, what should I do?* Babe just stayed there, thinking of how filthy she felt and how ashamed she felt. She felt too ashamed to call or tell anyone. She finally got up and ran some bathwater and washed herself off. She then lay in bed, crying and thinking how she was going to be ready for the exam and what she would do. Babe realized that if she didn't call the police and report to them, this man may continue to do this and get away. She then called the police and reported the incident.

It wasn't long before a couple of officers were there taking a report. Babe told the officers what had happened. As the officers investigated the home, they saw that he had cut the phone wires in the living room, but he didn't know about the one in Babe's bedroom. The living room had a lower window that had been taken out, and because the man wasn't that big, he must have crawled through the window after pushing the stereo out of the way. Babe had forgotten to turn the porch light on.

After she finished giving them the report, one officer told her she needed to go to the hospital for a specimen exam.

"What's that?" Babe wanted to know. She said OKAY, but when the officer found out she had taken a bath, he told her it was too late. Babe didn't know she had washed the evidence away. The officers told Babe she needed to come down and identify some mugshots. Maybe she would recognize this person, so they left Babe the information for her to come later.

Babe was exhausted after the officers left, but she decided to call Patrick. Patrick came over and comforted her. He knew she was planning to go to Oklahoma City within two days. She didn't know if she should, but she had already paid her money for the test, and it was too late for a refund, so she decided to go anyway. Patrick could see that Babe was troubled over the rape.

After the rape, Babe really began to think about protection. She had lived through too many burglaries, and she was too old to go back to living in the projects with her mother. Babe had made up her mind that she would buy herself a gun. Patrick decided to stay with Babe until she took the exam, and they would go to Oklahoma City together. He wanted to visit some friends while he was there.

On Saturday, Babe decided to visit the pawnshop and see what they had for protection. She picked out an automatic

.22caliber revolver. She purchased ammo to go with it, and at home, she loaded it and tucked it under her mattress.

On Monday, Babe and Patrick left for Oklahoma City early. She felt that ever since the man invaded her, she hadn't been able to study or concentrate. Patrick told her to try not to think about what happened. When they arrived at the testing site. Babe left the car with Patrick while she went in for the test; the exam would be anywhere from two to four hours. Babe figured she would need the entire four hours since she didn't test well, especially since she felt blank anyway.

After four hours, Patrick picked up Babe, and she told him she didn't think she did well, but they would let her know in about a week.

On the way home, Babe was still sad over what had happened. All the burglaries never scared Babe like the rape. She still liked living there since she had done so many improvements; she had even looked into building a pool. Babe was determined to stand strong. She didn't know anybody else to tell, and she didn't really need the therapy or the gossip. She managed to get by as she had, for Babe didn't want her immediate family to worry about her.

When they got back to Tulsa, Babe decided she wouldn't worry about it anymore. She wasn't working at the club, and she was about to switch to another day job. She decided before she went back to work at the nightclub, she would spend time looking for another day job since the one she was on left no room for advancement. Babe had been in the same department for five years since after high school.

Since Babe had worked for an oil company, she figured it would be nice to have a job with another oil company. Babe had a few applications out there; she was just hoping to hear from someone. Babe always found something to be thankful for. When she thought about the rape, she thought about how some don't live through them or some that were killed or beaten so bad they need medical and mental help. Babe felt fine, just a little shaken and ashamed, but not enough to let it get her down anymore. Patrick left Babe knowing she would be all right. He had made plans to catch a flight to Dallas, so he fixed Babe's bottom window and made sure everything was secure. Babe, determined not to let it get her down, put on a renewed strength, which energized her. She began to look forward to the start of a lot of good things going on.

Pam made her appearance every now and then since she didn't see Babe at the club anymore. She would stop by or call. Pam always had good gossip about the club, but when she stopped by this time, she could see Babe's mind was on something else. Finally, Babe opened up and told Pam what happened the week before. Pam could see Babe was trying to put it behind her. Babe told her she had to go to the police headquarters and look through some mugshots. Pam asked her when she had planned on doing it. As Babe thought about it, she figured as soon as she could; she needed to put some closure on the matter. Pam insisted that Babe hurry and get it out the way.

The next day, a female officer from the police department called Babe. Her voice was abrupt and loud, and her tactless manner upset Babe. The officer began to question her about the rape before she even identified herself. Babe asked her about the mug shots she was told about. The officer told her she needed to come down and review some pictures. Babe told the officer she would be right down.

Babe took the instructions the officer gave her, taking the elevator to the second floor. Turn right toward the bulletproof window. When she arrived, she met Detective Jones personally. Detective Jones asked her to have a seat as she pulled out the albums.

While Babe looked through the mug shots, the detective asked Babe if she knew the guy, and Babe told her that she didn't know him. Page after page, Babe was getting concerned because it seemed like so many of them. As Babe looked through the pictures, she glanced at least a hundred times. She didn't know if she could be sure.

About the time she finished, she noticed a picture that she thought had some resemblance. Babe went over the picture again, and she thought for sure, this one guy stood out. It was just a week ago, and Babe didn't know for sure, but she had identified someone that fit his description. When she pointed the picture out to the detective, she grunted as if she were annoyed. She didn't tell Babe what the guy had been accused of before; she didn't seem like she cared at all. She had asked Babe again if she knew the guy, and for the third time, Babe told her no. After it was over, Babe felt as though she was the criminal.

When the details behind the mug shots were over, Babe thought about the advice the officer gave her about going to a clinic. Since it would take a few days before she could see a doctor, she decided to drive over to the clinic. When Babe explained the problem, they ushered her in. She was told the doctor would call her back in a couple of days with the results, but the doctor assured her everything looked normal. They gave her a number for rape victims if she needed it. Babe figured she wouldn't pursue the case since she didn't know for sure that the picture, she identified was him. And since the help from headquarters wasn't solid enough to go on, she had to move on with other things.

A couple of weeks after the exam, Babe received a letter in the mail telling her that she didn't pass the exam. Babe wasn't surprised; she had felt blank when she was taking it. *Although Two Points Off Wasn't Too Bad,* Babe thought. Included in the letter was a list of dates for rescheduling, but Babe was too discouraged to think about going back.

Babe wasn't finished with the mail when she noticed a letter from an oil company where she had applied for a job in the accounting department. They were interested in her application and wanted an interview. Babe immediately called and scheduled the interview. The next day, she went to the interview, and during the interview, Babe shared her past experience and education. The supervisor was polite and listened intently, asking questions as they talked. The supervisor especially wanted the details about her working while in school through COE (Cooperative Office Education). Babe thanked him for the interview and left thinking no more about it. In fact, she applied for another job on the way home that evening.

At home, Babe felt depressed and decided to pull her Bible out. She opened it to Proverbs 3:5, one of her favorite verses. "Trust in the Lord with all your heart lean not to thy own understanding." Surely that was one on the top 10 list of scriptures. It seemed like there were many hurts and pains in the world, and no one understood but God.

Babe had heard that scripture as a child, but now it really meant something to her. To her, it was saying that if she trusted

God now, he would bring her through this trial. As she put the Bible away, the phone rang; it was the personnel office of the oil company, offering her the job for which she had interviewed. She was told the salary, and she immediately accepted. After she passed the physical, she would be ready for work. Her attitude had changed, and she had God to thank. Babe's first day at work renewed her totally. She didn't give up on the real estate; she just didn't want to tackle it again too soon.

At her new job, a few of the employees gathered around a bulletin board where they had posted photos from their childhood. They were laughing and joking about the photos. One girl asked Babe to bring her baby pictures. Babe was too embarrassed to explain that she had none. After work, Babe remembered the days in church when the pastor and his wife took pictures of her in the Easter pageant. Surely, they would have a picture of her somewhere.

Taking pictures was a great pastime for Babe, but she had mostly pictures of people and scenes—none from her younger days. Visiting this pastor took some courage since it had been before Babe became a teenager when Babe last saw him, then she drifted out of church. Babe knew they stayed in a house behind the new church. She convinced herself there was no harm in visiting them to see if they still had pictures. Pastor Morgan and his wife had retired now. But they still had that gentle spirit. Babe remembered how sweet both of them were. Their age had brought about senility, and they didn't remember Babe until she told them she was Barbara Johnson's daughter. Then they remembered Babe from church and other events.

Pastor Morgan wasted no time in asking Babe where she went to church. When she told him she was too busy working, he invited her to come back to Shiloh Baptist. Babe told him that since her mother attended there, she would like to find a church of her own someday. Babe didn't think she would feel independent enough if she were going to her mother's church. Not to mention she didn't want to go to church until she was ready. Babe grew up in a home where they had double standards, and she just didn't want to live the same way as when she went to church. Pastor Morgan just smiled and spoke. "A child shall lead them."

Together they searched their old photo albums, but there were no pictures of Babe. On Babe's way home, she stopped by Aunt Josephine's. Babe remembered Aunt Josephine keeping photo albums, so perhaps she would find some pictures there. Aunt Josephine had several picture albums, but not one held Babe's photo. It was disturbing to think no one kept one photograph of her.

"They Must Have Lost Them, Babe thought."

When she returned back to work, she heard them discussing the pictures. One lady said, "What a fun way to look back in history, at past events captured by a single sheet of paper."

Babe thought about the fashion-show pictures, but she didn't think they're as nice as having childhood-memory pictures. The fashion-show pictures were too glamorous.

Babe decided she would take more pictures of everything and everybody. She had a camera already, but it wasn't that good. So, she had made up her mind to purchase a better camera. She went directly to the pawn store and found a 35mm camera, with a carrying case and several lenses and filters that Babe knew nothing about. It wasn't long before Babe enrolled in a photography class at the junior college. She was thinking of using photography as a part-time job, and she needed to know all she could to make it work. Word got out that Babe was a camera buff. She received a few requests to take pictures in the club and special parties. There was no getting away from the club scene. Babe met a lot of people as she played the photographer. She made a few mistakes, but it was all in the learning and the fun of it.

Larry, the owner of Disco World, bumped into Babe at one of her parties, and he asked her when she was coming back to work. Larry told her that everybody missed her and would like to see her again. Larry pleaded with Babe since the last three waitresses didn't work out, and he knew he could depend on Babe. He offered her more money, and she was glad about that. Larry told Babe to call him or just come by the club. Babe didn't confirm that she would, especially after thinking about the rape. She didn't tell Larry about it, but she pondered on whether it happened because she had worked in the club. She reasoned with herself when she remembered reading about a girl coming home from church and got raped, when it had happened to her. Babe realized it could happen to anyone anywhere.

Babe reasoned with herself, "There are many perverts in the world." Before the week had ended, Babe called Larry and told him he could count on her. He was pleased because he knew Babe was a good waitress. The job gave Babe a positive outlook. Since she didn't have the bills, she had before, she was hopeful to save money now. The first night back at the club was like old times—the bartenders complaining about too many orders at one time, everyone talking, the music pounding as the floor seemed to be vibrating, the employee's agreeing to take turns having breakfast at different homes. The guys would buy the food, and the girls would cook.

At home, Babe's busy schedule resumed. One evening, she narrowly missed being hit by another driver, and they both came to a screeching halt. The gentleman got out of his car. Babe knew she had cut out too soon, and she was sure he would be angry.

"Are you all, right?" he asked with genuine concern.

She assured him she was fine and apologized. Babe was in a hurry and wasn't watching where she was going. Their cars were off to the side, and surprisingly, they simply began to talk as the traffic sped by them. In a matter of minutes, the sudden shock had transformed into a friendly acquaintance.

His name was Vince, and he seemed very interested in Babe. Vince wanted to contact her later about a date. After telling him about her schedule, Babe wondered if it seemed possible that he would be able to catch her. But they exchanged phone numbers just in case. Vince caught up with Babe the next day. He understood about her jobs and was tolerant of her busy schedule. Vince had a hectic schedule also. He was a foreign-exchange student in addition to working a full-time job. Babe assured Vince that her job at the club was safe, and the employees were like family, especially since she didn't see much of her own family. Actually, Babe and Vince began to spend more time together. They began doing things all the time. Vince knew when to call, and Babe really liked him. Vince lived with his brother and cousin; they're from Venezuela. They were all here to go to school; Babe liked learning about their culture. Babe thought Vince was hot, and she adored his curly black hair. She wasn't crazy about his thick bifocals, and he wasn't that tall, but she thought his intelligence made up for it.

Valentine's Day was approaching, and Babe wanted to do something special for Vince, so she invited him over for dinner and asked him to be her guest at the club. After dinner, he presented Babe with a gift, a book titled *"101 Ways to Make Money in Photography"*. At the club, Babe sat with Vince until his brother and roommate arrived, then she started work. Babe personally tended his table and gave them the red-carpet treatment. Larry noticed the special attention she was giving and asked jokingly what he had to do to be treated that way. All that week, Vince talked about what a good time he had and asked when she would invite him again. Babe told him he could come every weekend if he wanted.

Work at the club again became routine. Everyone was on Babe's case because she had stopped having breakfast afterward with them. Babe wouldn't get home until 6:00 am, and that was too late for her. Friday night at the club was as busy as ever. Babe waited patiently until the clock shifted to 2:00 am.

Her nights at the club were tiring at times, but nothing she hadn't been through before. It seemed like her job at the club had its highs and lows, especially since she wasn't able to drink—probably a good thing since it was easier to figure out if the customers had reached their limits. As she paced the dark aisle, clearly shouting "Last Call," she picked up her pace a bit, seemingly more anxious now that closing time was near. She watched security escort the people out, then she began counting her change, since she started with $20 and anything over that would be her tips. After counting $28, she figured at least she didn't lose any.

"Are you sure about that?" a voice behind her clearly stated.

As Babe looked behind her, she saw Edward, an ex-boyfriend trying to lure her out for breakfast. It was a nice thought, but Babe refused Edward's offer since she was dating Vince and she didn't want to seem like she was cheating on him. As Edward waved good night to Babe, he blew her a kiss and told her to call him. She signaled okay to him as she finished cleaning the place. She reminisced on how it had been with Edward. He was fun-loving and adventurous, but not the kind to settle down, Babe thought.

Finally, the doors closed. *I can now rush home to a relaxing bed,* she thought. Living a couple of miles from the nightclub gave her a short distance to travel. A light sprinkle still existed from an earlier rainstorm. Babe knew she had to be careful in the wet weather because of the wet streets and the narrowing curves could be an accident waiting. As Babe approached her home, she noticed a dark-blue Cadillac parked on the edge of a neighbor's curb, indicating that the neighbor might have guests. Babe was not aware that the car wasn't there by coincidence—a man was lurking around the corner, waiting for the right time to attack.

At 2:08 am, Babe was driving in the driveway. She liked the fact that she didn't have far for her part-time job. Every now and then, she would work the weekends, sometimes an extra day or so. Deep in her thoughts and wondering how she could avoid getting wet, Babe was totally oblivious to the fact that she was being watched.

Since it was still wet, Babe used her light jacket to shield her from the sprinkles still falling. She reached for her jacket to cover her head. Hurriedly she approached the porch to unlock the collection of locks on her door; the three locks made her feel somewhat safer since she had already experienced a few robberies.

Unlocking the last lock, she moved forward against the door, but it seemed to have opened much too easy, as if it were a push. As she looked behind her, the shock of seeing a man behind her was all too unsettling. As Babe tried to scream, his hand went over her mouth, and a struggle ensued. Near the door was a sectional couch, and the struggle caused them both to stumble over it. He then pulled out a long-bladed knife and held it to her throat. Now Babe's heart was racing in her chest; she was so afraid, she could hardly speak as she questioned him with a stuttering speech, "Who are you? What do you want?"

"Shut up and listen" he said in a raspy voice.

Babe felt the knife on her neck as he led her to the hallway and ordered her to take off her clothes. Babe tried to drag time out, but he could tell. He then ordered her down on the floor. The minutes seemed like hours; after he violated her body, he grabbed her from the floor and led her into the bedroom where she slept. He took the ski mask off her face and replaced it with a pillowcase. A ray of hope quickened Babe's thoughts as she remembered her .22caliber revolver under her mattress.

As he exited the room, all Babe could think about was holding the gun in her hand and detaining him for the police. Her hands felt for the gun, and she firmly embraced it. She yanked the pillowcase off her head, and, half-naked, grabbed a robe that was draped over the door, then she ran to catch this beast of a man.

He was leaving at the front door, but Babe held up the gun and ordered him to stop. Flashbacks of a previous attack on her life made her determined to avenge herself of this hideous experience. The guy was still in the living room, not yet out the door.

"Stop!" she yelled at him, fear in her eyes. Then she braced herself to shoot him. Ignoring her, he turned to leave. Carefully, with trembling hands, she positioned the .22caliber revolver and ordered him to stop. Again, he turned, and as his hand came out of his pocket, she envisioned him hurling the knife at her, and her fingers reacted by squeezing the trigger. The first bullet hit the window.

"My God!" she cried, then targeting him again, her panic power-emptied the gun. The man was in a heap on the floor. She ran back to the bedroom for more ammunition, then locked herself in the bathroom to reload the gun.

When she returned, he had crawled to the middle of the room and was crying for help. Finally realizing he could no longer hurt her, Babe then called for an ambulance. As she dialed, she could hear his pathetic cries for help.

"I wasn't going to hurt you," he wailed.

The dispatcher who answered the phone attempted to engage her in conversation until help arrived; she explained the situation to her while they waited. Her voice faded in and out as she mumbled several utterances, something about "Who's this man, why did he do this to me, now what am I going to do?"

"Are you all, right?" the voice on the phone asked.

"Sure, I'm just upset, I guess."

The officers arrived and were invited in after hanging up the phone. They questioned Babe as to his identity. Babe told the officer she didn't know him. They pulled his wallet out of his pants to identify him. As the officer flipped through the wallet, he pulled out some money and the officer mentioned that he had several hundreds on him.

Babe quickly responded, "He didn't get it from me."

At that moment, the ambulance arrived, and the paramedics got the rapist ready to go. A backup set of officers was to escort the ambulance. One officer told the paramedic, "Let me ride with you, I want to make sure he doesn't get away."

The other officers sat with Babe, and she went over the story. After writing everything in detail, they were ready to go, and they told Babe she would have to have a specimen test at the hospital. They asked Babe if she wanted to drive or if she would rather ride with them. She preferred to ride with them. It was so quiet you could hear a pin drop. Babe was still baffled over everything, and the officers didn't want to say anything to offend her, but they were soon at the hospital. It was better being escorted by the police officers; it seemed like it didn't take as long, and the next trip was downtown to talk to the district attorney. In a large conference room with a large table and some chairs, Babe waited by herself, and it seemed like the minutes turned into hours.

While Babe waited, she thought about her life, and for some reason, she knew that nothing would ever be the same. She thought about the rapist and wondered who he was, if he had family, or what would happen to him, then she silently prayed that he would be all right. As Babe asked for forgiveness from God, she pleaded earnestly because she knew she acted on instincts. Babe continued waiting and wondering what was taking so long. She wanted to leave but knew not to. *Maybe That's What They Wanted?* she thought. It was disturbing that she couldn't shed a tear and immediately started praising the Lord after asking for forgiveness. Then Babe prayed for the strength of God to deal with this. The night was long, and it seemed like morning would be longer. With her head still on the table, the officer finally knocked on the door and told her the district attorney would see her now.

Officer Green introduced Babe to the district attorney.

"Call me Ted," the DA said softly.

As they sat down, he apologized for the long wait and then asked her to review the story with him again. Following that, more questions were asked. When all was completed, Babe was informed that the rapist had died at the hospital. She was stunned but tried not to show any emotions in front of them. On the DA desk laid a folder that was stamped Justifiable Homicide. Then the case was closed.

"It's all over now," one of the officers told her.

"You can go home."

"Thank God," was all Babe could say.

The officer drove her home and tried to make her feel better by telling her how courageous she was. When they drove up to the house, Babe didn't feel very courageous; she felt like running away from it as fast and as far as she could. Too many horrible nightmares had taken place there. But she didn't run; she lifted her head high and walked in. Everything was clean; there was no blood on the carpet and virtually no sign of a struggle, although Babe noticed a small bullet hole in the glass of the front window that wasn't there before. Again, she thought of the dead man and began to cry. "I didn't want him to die." She sobbed as she realized it wasn't a bad dream; it really happened.

The ringing of the phone startled her. It was Edward. She explained to him what had happened; after Edward knew it was no joke, he commented, "Breakfast would have been better."

Call waiting allowed another call to interrupt the conversation. It was JJ, her brother. When she told him what had happened, he thought she was joking, but he soon realized that she wasn't joking about this. The tone was serious. Immediately, JJ and his wife, Joyce came right over. As soon as they arrived, the phone rang again. Joyce answered it. A local television station wanted to interview Babe. Joyce explained that Babe couldn't come to the phone.

After only a few minutes, another station called. Joseph Jr. suggested they go to their house. As they walked out of the house, the phone rang again, but this time they ignored it.

At JJ's house, Babe knew Vince would be trying to contact her, so she called him and told him what had happened. He was flabbergasted. Vince was the serious type, and he knew she was telling the truth. He told her how sorry he was and asked when he could see her.

"After work tonight," she told him.

Vince was upset, saying, "I can't believe you're going back to work."

"Why not? I've got to tell Larry what happened. I have nothing to be afraid of."

Vince was the reason Babe passed up breakfast with Edward. They had been dating about six months, and she didn't want Vince to think something was going on with her and Edward, so Babe decided not to tell Vince about her offer to have breakfast with an old friend. Babe sensed disappointment in Vince's voice as they hung up the phone. Larry, the owner of the club was especially nice to Babe; they'd worked together at another club when Larry was a security guard. He hired her at his club in a heartbeat, knowing she worked hard and was dependable. Babe grew despondent as she hoped Vince wasn't feeling second best to Larry; he had met him only a month ago when he and his brother visited for Valentine's Day.

Joyce and JJ could tell the heaviness Babe was feeling over the misfortune. JJ had overheard her tell Vince she was going back to work.

"If you didn't work at the club, this might not have happened," he said.

"That's not true," she countered. "Nine months ago, I wasn't working at the club. I was minding my own business, and someone entered my home and assaulted me." The fact that she was single and lived alone seems to make her easy prey for bad people. "But I bet they'll think twice before bothering me again," Babe stated.

JJ continued to talk against the waitress job at the club.

"Jesus went around sinners," Babe stated defensively.

"But you are not Jesus, and if you're not careful, that place will be the death of you."

"Then so be it!" she snapped. But after a few minutes, she recanted. "After tonight, I promise I'll think about quitting."

That evening, they watched the news together, and there was Babe's house on TV. The newscaster was telling all about the justifiable homicide. Thankfully, no name was ever mentioned, but all her friends knew her house. JJ joked about her being a celebrity, but somehow it just wasn't funny. They tried to talk her out of going to work, but when they saw it was useless, they let her go.

Later that evening, Babe left. She wanted to change clothes and meditate before going to work. At the club, she told Larry the whole story. He asked if there was anything he could do. He suggested accompanying her home to check the house, but she told him she wasn't going straight home. He insisted that he at least walk her to her car. Babe agreed to that, thanking him ahead of time.

Babe wanted to leave after letting Larry know, but she decided to wait it out. The disco lights were rotating wildly, or was it just in Babe's mind? As every step grew heavier, she felt the unease of people watching her. Multiple-colored lights revolving around the disco dance floor made the room appear as if it were spinning, causing her head to ache without any sign of relief. The first customer she waited on knew about it. He was a friend of a cousin. He blundered over his words, saying something like, "I heard you were raped last night."

"He didn't live to talk about it," she shot back.

Seeming to be confident in what she said, she didn't skip a beat as she continued serving the customers. Her coworkers were a comfort, but she could feel the tension among the customers.

After work, Larry escorted Babe to her car. There she informed Larry she wouldn't be back. He was sad, but he knew that she had to do what she felt best. Vince would be waiting for her at his apartment; she felt strange and watched closely that no one followed her. She was glad Vince was watching out the window and came out to meet her as she drove up. He greeted her with a hug.

"I heard all about it on the radio and the paper. You're a hero," he said.

His brother and roommate were eager to hear the story. Her voice trembled as she shared the humiliating experience. They were supportive with hugs and joked about getting an autograph. Vince was planning to return to Venezuela within two weeks and asked her if she would go back with him. The thought of leaving Tulsa sounded good, but still upset about the rape, she couldn't bring herself to take that chance. Babe didn't think that leaving would erase what had happened, and she thought maybe Vince felt sorry for her, not really loving her, but the thought of Vince asking her made her think that perhaps Vince really cared and was special. Still, she wouldn't go. She knew she had to deal with the situation herself. With all the commotion going on, Vince and Babe saw little of each other before he left, but he promised he would write.

Babe's entire family became very concerned for her. After she quit the club, she agreed to live with her sister Josie for a time. While gathering clothes to take to Josie's house, her neighbor Nancy stopped by to visit. She said she wanted to have a word of prayer. She had heard about the rape-murder. Nancy had always been a good neighbor, and of all the neighborhood children, hers were the best. Since she lived right next door, Babe considered her a good friend. Nancy had recently made a conversion in her faith and was Pentecostal. As she prayed, it seemed like God was present. Babe listened to her speak to God, and she felt her concern. Nancy's prayer strengthened Babe.

After she finished praying, Babe asked her if her guest had left. Nancy didn't know what she was talking about.

"There was a car in front of your house the night it happened." Babe thought she had a guest staying overnight. It was then that they realized the car belonged to the rapist.

Nancy stood to leave. "It wasn't your fault," she assured Babe. "Stay strong in the Lord." When she learned, Babe was going to stay with her sister for a while she said, "May God be with you."

At Josie's house, dinner was being placed on the table. Babe always enjoyed Josie's cooking, but she had no appetite. She put her things away while they ate. Afterward, she helped Josie clean the kitchen, and they talked.

"I only want to stay a few days," Babe said.

Josie patted her shoulder. "Stay as long as you like, Babe."

Later, she was laying her clothes for work the next day, and Josie looked at her. "What's that for?" she wanted to know.

"Clothes for work."

"You're not going to work, I hope."

"Look," she said firmly, "I've quit one job, you don't expect me to quit the other one, do you?"

"Of course not, but you could take a few days off."

"I don't need to take any time off," Babe said.

"Whatever you say." Josie shook her head and walked off.

Afterward, the house was quiet. Babe lay down on the couch and wondered about the commandment in the Bible that says, "Thou shall not kill." She whispered a prayer to God to forgive her then fell fast asleep and slept well.

Waking up early was a practice of Babe's. However, listening to kids fighting and fussing wasn't the best thing to wake up to. Josie had cooked breakfast, but Babe still had no appetite. As she dressed, she wondered if her coworkers had heard the news as yet. She knew she would have to face them sooner or later; it might as well be now.

At work, she arrived about ten minutes early. The place was quiet; a few of the workers were busy preparing for their workday.

Alice, a close friend at work, came in. When she saw Babe working, she exclaimed, "What are you doing at work?"

"I'm a paid employee here, just like you, remember!"

With tears in Alice's eyes, she stated how she'd seen Babe's house on the news and had heard the whole story. Looking into her tear-filled eyes, Babe quipped, "I should be the one crying."

They both laughed, breaking the awkwardness of the moment. It was sort of strange. Before all this happened, Alice jokingly used to call Babe a child prodigy. Babe never figured out why—maybe Alice was reading too many books? Now she was commending her for her courage and told her how proud she was of her.

"Please let me know if there's anything I can do for you," she added with a smile.

When everyone else had arrived, the whispering among the employees was more than obvious. One girl shouted out, "Etta, was that you that killed that guy?"

Without thinking, Babe said, "I could write a book," inwardly thinking that would answer the entire story.

Throughout the day, visitors were browsing the area, and Babe was aware of the different expressions and reactions from both fellow employees and the public. Even her supervisor had a peculiar stare. She began to look forward to the noon hour and the chance to get away. Just as Alice and Babe were leaving for the cafeteria, the phone rang. It was a reporter.

"KTEW, Ms. Johnson. I've tried to catch you at home, I just want to ask you a few questions, and it won't take very long," Babe heard the voice say. Hoping to keep them off her back, Babe granted her a short interview over the phone. After the series of questions were completed, the reporter asked Babe if she was religious, quickly Babe responded no. Within minutes of hanging up, guilt set in. Babe knew she had been a believer all her life but to say she was religious just didn't fit. Babe felt terrible and asked

Alice to excuse her while she went to the restroom; there she had a chance to recant. "Oh, Lord, forgive me if it seemed like I was denying my belief in you, you alone give me strength and hope." Babe held the cross around her neck; she knew it was deeper than she could explain.

Lunch didn't have much appeal, and a small bowl of soup was more than enough. As they ate, Alice asked how long Babe would live with Josie.

"Not long, I hope."

While Alice talked, Babe's mind wandered about things elsewhere. Scenes at the club crossed her mind. During one particular time, a gentleman had asked her where her man was, and she boldly held the crucifix before him and proclaimed, "Here he is." *Could it be that I am supposed to be a nun?* thought Babe.

A little shaken by her thoughts since Babe was baptized in the Baptist Church at a very young age, the fear of being a nun didn't settle well with her. Neither did the idea of being Catholic sound right to her. She didn't go to church, but for some reason, Babe had a habit of wearing a cross around her neck. This was more or less to identify her belief in Christ even though her lifestyle wasn't exactly what you would call holy. Babe believed that God loved her, and with time, she would totally commit to him. She didn't feel ready to go to church; she had hoped to be married first before committing to a church.

The next day, the *Oklahoma Eagle* came out with an article that identified the attacker as having a past history of rape. It revealed information that wiped away all the awful rumors that were being circulated.

In the *Tulsa World*, it said that the rapist had been under police surveillance. Babe found herself wondering where the police were when he was stalking her. It didn't matter since the truth did prevail.

Staying at Josie's turned out to be longer than she had expected. One evening, Babe stopped by her place to pick up a few things. A classmate who worked in a hospital had barely caught Babe in time to give her an orchid that a doctor had sent to Babe. They talked for a while then departed. On her way to Josie's, Babe was overwhelmed by all the people that felt sorry for her and kind of resented it even though she knew they meant well. She kept mulling over it. "Lord, I don't want their pity."

By now Vince was in Venezuela, and Babe was trying to put him out of her mind, thinking maybe that it was his way of walking out on her forever. Even though he said he would write, somehow Babe thought that it was just an alibi, and she was sure she'd never hear from him again. Nevertheless, Babe couldn't worry about Vince; she knew Josie was waiting, and she didn't want to keep her waiting. Just as Babe arrived at Josie's, the phone rang. It was her mother.

"How are you doing?" the voice spoke.

"Fine. Josie is making me feel very welcome here," she told her mother. As a matter of fact, Babe told her mother she was thinking about her on the way over because she used the travel bag they had when they were vacationing awhile back.

Babe's mother wasn't big on talking, and Babe found herself making conversation.

Mother spoke again, "You be careful."

Their conversation came to an end, and now with her luggage unpacked, she could relax and grab a bite to eat.

Malcolm, Josie's husband, traveled a lot with his job as a truck driver for a local food chain. Even when he was in town, he knew Babe like a sister himself. Josie appeared to be blessed with a loving husband as well as a healthy son. She didn't work other than being a housewife and a mother, which seems to be the ideal job. Josie lived only a couple of miles away, which was probably why she and Babe seemed to be the closest in the family. James called from California to see if Babe was okay, and Martin, their brother, called Joseph to see if everything was okay. Candi still lived in Tulsa; they didn't visit much, but she did call to see if Babe needed anything.

When Josie saw Babe's carry-on luggage emptied, Josie thought an overnight bag would have been fine. Josie jokes, looking a little disappointed.

Babe trembled as she responded, "Josie, please let me stay a week. I'm going through something, and I don't want to be alone."

Josie smiled, and her expression seemed to reassure Babe that it was okay. The week passed by fast.

Malcolm and Josie's son was six years old; he enjoyed spending time with Malcolm's family—his uncles and aunts along with a host of cousins. Malcolm's family was close, and Josie liked it. Markie was a little spoiled, being the only child; plans for Markie to spend the weekend with Malcolm's family gave Josie and Babe plenty of time to shop. Babe wasn't big on shopping, but Josie loved to go from store to store, sometimes not buying a thing. For Babe, it was just a pastime.

As Babe prepared herself for work the next day, she listened as Josie responded to a phone call she received from Malcolm. It sounded like Malcolm would be coming in early, probably by Thursday or Friday, and he would be home for the entire weekend.

There go plans for shopping, Babe thought.

Babe knew she didn't want to wear out her welcome knowing that Josie and Malcolm had been trying to have another child. She didn't want to deprive them of their time together.

Josie wanted more children, and the doctors told her she had a few extra fiber tissues in the way, but with time, it could happen. Since Malcolm was due in by the end of the week, Babe prepared to leave that Wednesday.

Chapter 4

A Different Horizon

Time away from Babe's home was appreciated and gave her peace. Spending time with loved ones gave her some comfort as well, but she was ready to return to her home. She moved back into her house, and the memories of what had happened didn't bother her as much, and the idea of regaining her privacy was comforting. The house was dusty and dirty from her absence and in need of a thorough cleaning.

Babe stopped by the supermarket for cleaning supplies, and while there, she was moved to see an old classmate, whom she had a crush on while in high school.

"Clarence is that really you?" she said with disbelief. They both agreed how they had changed a great deal since their school days.

"Are you seeing anyone?" he wanted to know.

First thinking about Vince and then realizing he was gone, she responded, "Not really." "Let's get together," he suggested.

Babe gave him her home number, hoping Clarence would call her soon.

On the way home, Babe began to look forward to hearing from Clarence. *Perhaps this would be the person to fill the void Vince had left,* she thought. Clarence called that evening, and they talked for hours. She invited him over for a home-cooked meal at her place the next evening, and as they hung up, Babe wondered if he had heard about what had happened. She was afraid to mention it for fear it would scare him off, but then she decided it would be better for him to hear it from her. Babe decided she would tell Clarence herself. The next day, she hurried home from work to prepare dinner. The phone was ringing as she approached the door. She stumbled through her keys, trying to get to the phone before it stopped ringing. It was Clarence, but she couldn't concentrate on what he was saying. Things were rearranged in her living room; items were missing. Babe had been robbed again! She interrupted Clarence to explain that her place had been burglarized. He offered to come right over. Calling the police began to be a redundant practice.

Two officers arrived in separate cars. They instructed her to take account of everything missing for the insurance company. They discovered the bars had been taken off the back window again, and the garage was used as an escape exit. They continued investigating while Babe paced the floor, thinking how she could continue living at her home. Babe told the officers about the rape and justifiable homicide that she had recently lived through. They verified what she said and mentioned moving to her. The thought of moving sounded good, but she had a mortgage on her house and didn't want to lose it. Reporting burglaries were a practice that was getting very old; in fact, she was sick of it.

Preparing dinner was no longer on her mind. After the officers left, Clarence arrived and offered to take her out to eat. He ordered a steak, but all Babe wanted was a glass of tea. She was worried that the matter was getting out of hand. Perhaps now was as good a time as any to tell Clarence, as he finished his dinner. Slowly she explained about the past burglaries, the two incidents of rape, the killing, and now this. Clarence took the toothpick from his mouth and laid it on the plate.

"Would you like me to stay with you for a while?" he asked.

The invitation made her uncomfortable, but fear forced her to give in. "Thanks," she answered. "I would like that." She didn't want to continue imposing on Josie.

Back at the house, Clarence's company made her feel somewhat safer. As they straightened up the mess, they talked of old times. He then told her he had a two-year-old son. He explained about his son's mother and how he discreetly broke up with her. Babe sensed he missed them.

"They're back in Hawaii where they're from." Clarence reached over and kissed her and assured her that she was beginning to fill the emptiness in his life.

It was obvious that Clarence still cared for his son and his son's mother, and for that reason, Babe secretly vowed not to fall for him too quickly. She didn't exactly fear for her life, but she still sensed trouble, and she didn't want to defend herself again, so his presence was buying her time for now. That evening, they shared about their work. Clarence was a shop worker at the manufacturing plant located about three miles from where he lived. He stayed in a duplex not far from Babe's place, about seven miles from where she lived. He told Babe about his Doberman pinscher named Danger. Danger was still just a pup, but Clarence hoped one day he would be a good guard dog. As the evening grew late, Babe knew that if they didn't get any sleep, they both may not be able to work effectively on their jobs the next day.

Babe didn't want to tell Clarence about the abortion since she didn't think it would matter; she knew she didn't want to be intimate with Clarence and wondered if he would understand. Before showing Clarence to the bedroom, Babe told Clarence. She wanted to wait instead of rushing into sex.

"I'm mentally not ready to engage in a sexual relationship."

Clarence hesitated but then agreed. "It will be better when you are ready."

That night, they cuddled in each other's arms as they slept. Babe felt secure while she silently prayed.

The alarm clock woke them up early. Five was routine with Babe, sometimes earlier. Clarence wasn't into waking so early, but since he had to go home before he could prepare for work, he struggled to stay up. While Babe prepared herself, Clarence made conversation.

"I'll bring Danger over tonight."

"That will be fine." Babe thought that it was a good idea, and from his place, she could go to work. Babe followed Clarence as he left the driveway. It only took fifteen minutes to reach Clarence's place, and since Babe was still about an hour and a half ahead of her schedule, Clarence offered her coffee to drink while he prepared himself for work. His duplex was a 2-bedroom duplex, which he leased from his grandmother, who raised him.

The smell of Danger was eminent; Danger was big for his age. He playfully jumped on Clarence, and Babe could see he was far from being dangerous as his name claimed. Clarence made a good cup of coffee. Danger licked Babe's hand as she reached out to pet him. With about forty-five minutes before work, Babe decided to leave to be on time. Clarence demanded a hug before she left, and he assured her not to worry, promising her that he would be at her place between six or seven that evening.

At work, the first thing Babe needed to do was to notify the insurance agent. The insurance had only saved Babe once because the deductible wasn't enough to be bothered with, but this time, it seemed like there was much more damage as well as loss. The receptionist put her on hold as she waited to be transferred to an insurance adjuster.

"Kyle Thomas," the voice answered.

"Mr. Thomas, my name is Valleta Juanetta Johnson, and I have insurance with your company. I need to report a burglary yesterday. The police were called out and I have a report."

"Ms. Johnson, we need to appoint an adjuster to estimate the claim."

"That is why I called," Babe said.

"What about Tuesday around 9:00 am. I will meet you personally."

"That will be fine."

Immediately, Babe made plans with her supervisor to be late that Tuesday. She had to explain why Mr. Turner hired her a year ago and had always felt that Babe was reliable and never abused her privileges. Even though Babe felt suspicious of many man made tests that she probably didn't pass, she resented being put on trial by man to test her trustworthiness.

Alice was anxious to hear why Babe was in the supervisor's office. She observed while Babe seriously took care of matters that she didn't know about. Work had been delayed as Babe made sure arrangements were made. Now she silently sorted the tickets to catch up.

Alice, sitting next to Babe, mentioned, "Are you going to tell me, or is it any of my business?"

Babe looked at Alice as she worked. "Let's talk about it during lunch."

It was agreed that they would have lunch together. During lunch, Babe caught Alice up on everything within those two days of changes. Alice was glad to hear about Clarence, but she feared Babe didn't really like him. He seemed convenient for her at the time.

Alice mentioned Vince, and Babe shunned her, saying, "I miss Vince, but I'm not sure if Vince will return. Don't worry. I think Clarence is missing his son and baby momma. And it may be that he's buying time as well."

After work, Babe hurried home, wanting to surprise Clarence with a well-prepared meal, which he missed the other day. As she checked her mail, there was a letter from a lady in Nebraska. Babe didn't recognize her name. In the letter was a check for $100. She was amazed that someone cared enough to offer her money.

On the check was a telephone number, and the name on the check read Rosemary Wells. Babe read the letter. Rosemary seemed concern about Babe; she had been following her life since the rape, and she had read the paper and read about the burglaries as well. In her letter, she expressed a desire to help her. Babe thought it was appropriate to call Rosemary and thank her. She dialed the number and asked for Rosemary. It sounded like a housemaid had answered the phone. Rosemary was summoned to the phone. Babe introduced herself and thanked her for the money. Rosemary asked Babe if she wanted to move to another place, and if so, she would help her move. It was kind for Rosemary to make this generous offer. Babe didn't know how she could explain that she now had a friend living with her and that she would be all right.

When Babe told Rosemary about Clarence staying with her now, there was silence on the line. Babe could tell by the silence that she didn't approve of the situation. Babe broke the silence by suggesting that they have dinner together some time.

"I seldom accept dinner invitations," Rosemary said. "But I'll consider having tea with you at my condominium next time I'm in town. Usually, I'm pretty busy on my two-hundred-acre ranch, but let's keep in touch."

Talking with Rosemary had Babe thinking seriously about a move. This thing with Clarence was a comfort for her now because of what she had just lived through, but she didn't know if it was right to jump into a relationship. Even though she was attracted to Clarence, she thought perhaps she didn't think it through.

While she prepared dinner, she thought of what she would do with her house. The option of leasing her house was an idea. With a mortgage hanging over her head, she couldn't just move out.

Dinner wasn't anything special since Babe hadn't shopped for groceries, but even tuna casserole and vegetables would make a meal, she thought.

Clarence arrived just as the meal was ready. Danger was with him. Babe was glad that Clarence let Danger stay outside while they ate. Babe told Clarence about Rosemary's letter and her wanting to help Baby move. Clarence told her how he couldn't believe a total stranger would help and how he would hate for her to give up her home.

"The house is almost haunted now. I've lived through countless nightmares, and I don't think it's worth giving up my peace of mind," Babe said.

"What will you do with your house?" Clarence asked.

"The possibility of leasing it out sounds okay."

After dinner, Clarence let Danger in to protect them—at least that is what he said. They continued discussing the idea of Babe moving. Finally, Babe admitted to Clarence.

"How long do you think this might last?"

Clarence looked awkward. "What do you mean?"

"I know that you still miss your family, and I know they will always be first in your life."

Clarence looked away, not knowing what to say. "If this is your way of saying you don't want me, don't blame it on my family. They're gone, and I'm here all alone. It's not a crime to want someone for me now."

Babe confessed to Clarence, "I truly don't know what I want, Clarence. I don't want to use you for my safety. The thought of having someone here seemed like a good idea, but I don't know where we're going with it. I was involved in a relationship before I met you. Vince wanted me to follow him back to Venezuela. I don't think I'll hear from him again, and I don't know if I'm ready for another relationship."

Clarence approached Babe, embracing her in his arms. "I'll be whatever you want for now, if you need protection, I'm here, as well as a friend."

It seemed right having Clarence there even though Babe felt the situation was unpredictable. The more he held her, the more she desired him.

At bedtime Clarence's warm body comforted her, and his advances grew more inviting. Babe halted his move as she explained, "I cannot.

As he shifted his body to see her speak, he asked,

"Why? Does it bother you because of the rape now?" Babe stated softly, "I don't want to rush."

At night, it seemed longer than ever, knowing that Clarence was anxiously waiting. However, the thought of being with Clarence sexually was becoming harder to avoid. *Things are happening too fast,* Babe thought. *Maybe That's why the relationship is going too fast. We're living together like husband and wife.*

As she realized what she had got into, she began to see her mistake. Clarence gave her space, not wanting to rush Babe; he could see she was going through something. He became supportive of whatever she wanted. As she talked about moving, he could see that she was serious.

On Sunday, Clarence awoke thinking about church, hoping Babe would attend church with him. Clarence's and Babe's grandmothers attended the same church. But Babe wasn't interested. Clarence attended alone. After Clarence left, Babe silently thought about God. She didn't know why she didn't want to attend church; she believed in God and always prayed. She reminisced about her childhood experience with God and her baptismal at a very young age. "How dare you condemn the sinner, Jesus's blood paid for her sins"—her words at the first Easter pageant that marked her as an elect of God. At the tender age of seven years old, Babe seemed to know how to please the Lord.

Her personal commitment to wear a cross always identified her belief in Christ, but now she wondered if it had caused part of her problems in life.

Before dating Vince, Babe remembered a short relationship she had with a very wealthy guy that lived in Chicago. He was an atheist. And they argued about things that seem irrelevant, but Babe believed that he picked things to argue about because he didn't like it when she wore her cross.

Al blamed God for retarded children, but Babe denied that God was responsible, and not knowing the Bible that well, Babe didn't know how to defend God; but she didn't let it keep her from collecting her hearts and crosses. Babe and Al eventually broke up; the nice gifts weren't worth the risk of denying God.

Babe knew that her lifestyle wasn't perfect, but she knew that she didn't harbor hatred in her heart for anyone, and she never met anyone she didn't like. At least that's the way she tried to be, but the way the churches needed money, it would probably be another bill for her at that time, and she was trying to pay off some bills. Babe knew that it was scripture to give to the church and she didn't want to be a freeloader, but in time, Babe felt that she would commit to a good church. Her old classmate and friend Mary had been praying for her.

Mary used to be a Catholic, but she switched to Pentecostal. Babe wanted to have a relationship with God and didn't want to be in bondage to what appeared to be in some churches. Then she started thinking about the abortion, wondering whether God had forgiven her. She had prayed about it and felt his peace, but the churches called it murder.

Killing a rapist is one thing but having an abortion—some people would want to condemn her to hell for both, she thought. Suddenly, an urge to read the Bible appeared to be a good idea. Babe reached for the Bible and prayed for God's understanding. As she began to read Psalm 23, she knew that the Lord was her shepherd and that he would lead her through the still waters. Babe felt so thankful, thinking about all that God had allowed her to live through. Shortly after the first rape incident, she read about a young lady walking to church and was raped. That proved to Babe that working at a nightclub wasn't the reason for the rape. After reading the Bible, she felt that it was a good sermon directly from God. Clarence was returning from Church with his Bible in his hand. When he entered the door, it looked like gloom had hit him instead of a spiritual uplift.

Babe questioned Clarence, "What's wrong? You didn't like the sermon?"

Clarence responded, "It's okay, I guess, it just seems like they preach money all the time. I don't remember the sermon."

Babe shared with Clarence how her Sunday sermon went at home.

"Sometimes I feel distant from the church. They have many dogmatic beliefs."

"What's dogmatic?" Clarence wanted to know.

"Sort of like twisting the law to say what they want it to say, like preaching mostly on giving instead of the love of God or condemning others for their sin."

Clarence suggested they go out to eat; he saw a friend and made plans to join him with his date after he picked Babe up. Clarence insisted that Babe get ready.

"You remember Willet, our classmate?"

"How could I forget Willet?"

Clarence had spoken of him all the time. They had grown up together and attended the same church. They all graduated in the same class. Willet was a little in the fast lane. Babe remembered a hot romance he shared in high school with a neighborhood friend; she became pregnant and was now raising Willet's son.

"Who's the date for Willet?"

"His longtime girlfriend, now his fiancée. Willet is getting married. They haven't planned the date, but they're serious."

At the restaurant, Willet and his date were waiting. The waitress ushered Babe and Clarence to the table. Willet recognized Babe and was glad to see her. Babe remembered the last time she saw Willet and his fiancée; they're at a nightclub where Babe was taking pictures of a fashion show. They immediately struck up a conversation about the fashion show and the pictures Babe took of Willet and Sharon. Babe remembered them both.

Before dinner, they talked about high school and old friends. Willet was a music teacher at a local high school, and Sharon's father taught Babe in a woodcraft class. Babe told them about the tables she was still using that she had made in her summer class. After dinner, Clarence wanted to visit his family. On the way home, he stopped by and introduced Babe to his cousins, uncle, and aunt. They didn't live far from Babe's place.

They were all glad to see Clarence and entertained him with a game of dominoes. Babe played as Clarence's partner. She admitted that she hadn't played lately and was rusty. Clarence bragged that he would cover her. Tony, Clarence's cousin partnered with his father, Clarence's uncle. The game was going smooth until Tony asked Clarence if he had heard from Christine, Clarence's son's mother.

Clarence admitted that he received a letter from her last week. With all ears opened, Babe heard and began to wonder why he hadn't said anything to her about it.

Tony insisted, "How is she doing?"

"Wanting money, as usual," Clarence responded.

Babe wondered if Clarence had told his family anything about what Babe had just lived through. A lot of the talk was just general, other than talking about Clarence's family in Hawaii.

Clarence and his uncle stood. As Clarence grabbed his wrap, Babe could see they would be leaving. Tony and his uncle both welcomed Babe to come back anytime, boasting that the next game would be theirs.

As Clarence drove, he asked Babe, "Did you have a good time today?"

"You made my weekend," Babe assured him. She mentioned that she and Josie would have been hanging out doing nothing, but her outing with Clarence was refreshing, especially after seeing Willet, their old friend.

Clarence reached over to hold Babe's hand. Babe proceeded to tell Clarence what her agenda would be like that week—her appointment with the insurance adjuster and how she feared they wouldn't give her what her valuables were worth. She told Clarence she only collected once, when she had a roommate, and how the roommate wanted her to pay for her things with the insurance money. Babe told her that she was going to adjust the rent for her roommate, but she became upset about it and moved. The insurance company didn't give her much to start with, and her roommate wanted her stereo and jewelry replaced. Babe grew upset about losing a roommate and a friend but was leery about the situation since she was having an affair with Babe's sister-in-law's husband. The insurance didn't kick through for all the other burglaries Babe experienced because the deductible was too high.

Tuesday wasn't long in coming, and Babe was seeing Clarence off to work. It was sort of good to have Danger there; he appeared to be good company as Babe waited for the insurance adjuster to arrive.

Babe went over the list of items that was taken, trying to remember if there was anything else. Serial numbers and receipts were located to be attached with the police report, which the police left with her.

About 8:45 am, the door knocked. Babe hoped it was the adjuster; she didn't want to wait too long. At the peephole, she noticed a tall white man holding a briefcase. She figured that he had to be the adjuster.

As the door opened, she asked him to identify himself. "Kyle Thomas, insurance adjuster."

Babe welcomed him in. First, they went over the details of the burglaries, and she gave him a list of all the missing items along with the police report.

Kyle glanced around the house with admiration for her decorating style, and as he complimented her, he asked, "Do you live alone?"

Catching Babe off guard, she didn't know how to identify Clarence since he had just moved in, and she wasn't sure about it all. With a feeling of faith, she responded, "My boyfriend moved in after the burglary."

As he wrote his notes, he confirmed her address. "4120 N. Franklin Avenue," and suddenly, it dawned on him the event that must have happened over a month ago. "Did you hear about the woman on the north side that killed a rapist? Wasn't that somewhere around here?" he asked.

Shocked that he would ask about that, Babe couldn't hold back, "That was me, and now another burglary."

"Wow, you killed the guy." Babe tried to defend herself; she mentioned that she was tired of all the burglaries and that was the second rape she had experienced. "I was forced to buy a gun."

Kyle marveled at her as she talked. "I don't blame you," he said. With all the details recorded, Kyle asked her if he could look around. He toured outside the house and through the garage, making a note of all the dead bolts.

When he returned, he told Babe his assignment was over, and he would contact her within two or three weeks for her claim. As he turned to leave, he mentioned the weather being nice, suggesting a nice day to move. Babe smiled to let him know she got the point.

Babe let Danger out before locking up; she didn't want to come home and see everything torn apart. The adjuster was prompt, and she appreciated that since she knew she had to be at work. Babe was conscientious of being late, and she was glad she could still make it to work by 11:00 am.

At work, everyone was busy preparing for lunch, and since she arrived late, she decided not to take lunch. While working, Babe thought about what the adjuster said regarding moving. It seemed like everyone had the same idea. Even Clarence began to accept it. Maybe moving would make the difference. As she thought about it, a plan to make a move started rolling. Anxiously, Babe planned to pick up application forms along with a newspaper to seek what the market was for renting. Not only would she be renting her house out, but she would also be looking for a place to rent.

After lunch, everyone returned except Alice. Babe hadn't noticed before if Alice was at work. She figured that she would be all ears, wanting to know what had happened. Curiously, Babe asked Sandy,

"Is Alice in today?"

"No, Alice called in sick today."

Babe couldn't remember Alice saying anything about being sick. Babe wondered if something was wrong. Alice didn't call in sick much, leaving Babe to worry about her. Not wanting to take away her time from work, she planned to call Alice after work.

Leasing her house would be a new experience. At home, Babe reached for her real estate book—basically a book from the last class she took—thinking she could pick up some pointers. A section about landlords caught her attention, but nothing about how to lease; it seemed like practical knowledge would have to teach her.

Babe purchased application forms and lease agreements at the office supply store. The forms were sold separately and didn't cost much, one of each, and then she could duplicate them and save money.

At home, Clarence was looking through the paper when Babe walked in. She mentioned, "Save the Classified ads, I'm looking for an apartment."

The newspaper had listed several apartments, and it pleased Babe to learn that rent for an apartment would be much less than what she was paying on her mortgage note, which meant she could lease her house for a higher price.

Clarence and Babe looked through the Classified ads together. The nicer apartments were on the south side, which didn't bother Babe because she worked out south. Even Clarence began to sound excited about it. Clarence suggested he assist her in moving, which pleased Babe.

Move or lease—Babe didn't know what order it should happen. She knew she had to lease her home first. Since she couldn't place an ad to lease until the weekday, Babe thought it would be nicer for her and Clarence to go sightseeing.

None of the apartments in the paper seemed to interest Babe; instead, they decided to look around to see what the neighborhoods were like. They came upon one neighborhood that seemed secluded. The entire area was a cluster of apartments; they were all clean and well-kept. Deep in the seclusion was a group of condominiums. Royal Palace, the billboard identified. For some reason, they appealed to Babe. It looked as if the clubhouse was open, so they parked the car to check it out.

The clubhouse was nice and cozy, with an upstairs loft. Babe hadn't lived in apartments much, so she didn't know what to look for, and the atmosphere was nice. Inside the clubhouse, a lady appeared to be leaving. She looked like the receptionist. Babe asked her about a one-bedroom vacancy.

"Upstairs or down?" she wanted to know.

"Is there a difference in price?" Babe asked.

"No."

"Then I'll look at an upstairs one first."

They followed the lady past the swimming pool and parking lot to a condo facing the clubhouse.

The receptionist unlocked the door, appearing to be for downstairs, but as they entered, they could see it was a stairway leading upstairs. They followed her up the stairs where the living quarters started. The rooms were spacious. The fireplace caught Babe attention. She had never lived in a place where there was a fireplace. The closet was big and roomy. Dishwasher, how nice, Babe thought.

Babe had completely made up her mind that she would enjoy living there. She asked the receptionist if she had any more available in case someone rented it before she could put a deposit on it. After assuring her that there was another one available, Babe and Clarence both left with a made-up mind. The thought of moving had Babe excited, and now she was ready to take the necessary steps to lease out her house.

With the weekend behind her, Babe was anxious to report to work, with plans to lease her house during her lunch hour. She completely forgot to call Alice over the weekend until she saw her at work that Monday.

"How are you?" Babe questioned.

"I'm okay, with the exception of being pregnant."

Pregnant! Babe looked at Alice to see her expression. She looked serious, and Babe asked her if congratulations were in order. Alice wasn't excited about it, but she feared another abortion. Her and Herb weren't married, but she decided to have the baby this time.

Alice's situation seemed a lot more serious than Babe's. They put off talking about it until lunchtime, and since Babe had planned to make a phone call at lunchtime, she explained to Alice they could meet later.

Placing an ad was of utmost importance. The ad agency told her the ad would appear as soon as the next day. Knowing if she got that behind her, everything else would fall in place. She brought the application and lease form to work to make several copies. While Alice waited, she ran the copies without anyone noticing.

In the cafeteria, with only fifteen minutes before lunch would be over, Babe joined Alice at her table.

Babe knew she didn't have time to eat.

"Well, fill me in," Babe said.

Alice seemed calm as she told Babe that she found out she was pregnant. She and Herb discussed having the baby because Alice didn't want to go through with another abortion. Alice looked upset because Herb wasn't ready to marry her. But she loved him, and nothing else mattered. As they prepared to return to work, Babe mentioned to Alice that she was making plans to move into some apartments not far from where she lived.

"First I have to lease out my house." Babe placed an ad during her lunch hour. "Just think, we're going to be neighbors, and if you need me, I can babysit for you."

The weeks following, Babe had accepted a young couple to lease her house. They had lived out of town prior to their move. With them planning to move in, Babe was preparing fast to move out. The condo that she liked was still available, and she was scheduled to move the same weekend the couple would be moving in. It didn't seem that it would be enough time, so Babe decided to schedule a day off. They had boxed up mostly everything, and Clarence had planned to use his company truck, along with his supervisor, Robert.

On Friday, Babe took over as many boxes as she could by car, along with her phone; she also arranged her telephone service and address to be switched. That evening, Clarence and Robert assisted with the heavier items. Babe gave a bedroom suite to Clarence. She had too much furniture. Candi, one of her sisters, had already taken some of the furniture. A girl at work bought her washer and dryer. The couple of loads were lighter since Babe had already gotten rid of the items, she wouldn't have room for.

After all the loads were emptied out of the house, Babe went through the house and cleaned as thoroughly as she could since the couple would be moving in that weekend.

Robert took the company truck back with him, and Clarence was in need of a ride.

Instead of leaving, he suggested he stay the night with Babe in her new apartment, and knowing she still needed her bed set up, Babe agreed that it would be a good idea.

Moving a bit of clutter, Babe and Clarence made their way to the bedroom, where he started putting her bed together. They both were tired and wanted to sleep, but the bed had to be assembled. He finished with the bed, and Babe didn't feel like putting any linen on it, but Clarence insisted on at least a sheet and spread. Clarence helped, and they were soon ready for sleep. Babe reached for a short housecoat, just taking off shoes and their street clothing, then they both lay close to each other. Babe held Clarence's hand as she thanked him; Clarence made an effort to say something but was soon asleep.

Sleeping late came easy for the both of them; Clarence awoke first. As he stared at Babe while she snuggled a pillow, he couldn't resist the desire to touch her, and as he wondered if she could be his, his body started caressing hers.

Before he knew anything, he was kissing her all over her body while she, half alert, responded. Clarence had aroused himself, and the feeling was mutual. Babe thought that she might miss him when he left. Clarence could tell he would have to be gentle with her; Clarence felt good that Babe was relaxing a bit more with him, and he felt that things would get better eventually.

Even for a quickie, he was comforted, thinking maybe the apartment was making a better change already.

That morning, he helped Babe unload boxes until everything was put in its proper place. He had to go back to his place and insisted that Babe join him. Babe pretended she had made plans with Josie, knowing she needed some time alone.

As she drove him home, he complained that she just didn't want to spend time with him.

"We've been together all week."

"What are you talking about?" Babe snapped.

"Okay, I'll see you later on."

After dropping Clarence off at his place, Babe decided it was a good time to visit Josie since they only talked on the phone briefly because Clarence was always over. Josie and Clarence both lived on the north side, and it would save on the gas for now. Now late in the afternoon, Babe figured everyone would be up, if not at home. Malcolm answered the door, seemingly somewhat surprised.

"Long time no see, stranger."

"You said it, and for how long."

"Where's Josie?"

Just as Babe mentioned Josie's name, she came with her apron on, insisting that Babe join her in the kitchen, where they all sat and caught up on new times. Malcolm questioned Babe and her relationship with Clarence and her new condo.

"Clarence is nice, but I think we're going too fast, and I can't stop it."

"You can't or you don't want to?"

"Something like that, I guess," Babe agreed.

"When do we meet him?" Josie suggested.

"Is tomorrow, okay?"

It was settled that Babe would bring Clarence over to meet Josie and Malcolm the next evening for dinner. After briefing them on her new home and giving Josie the address and her new phone number, Babe decided to leave; she didn't want to stay long since she didn't feel comfortable telling Malcolm about everything, and she didn't want him to excuse himself.

Babe thought, with all the extra time on her hands, she could browse the local pawnshop, where she would sometimes purchase things.

The downtown pawn shop was known to offer bargains from time to time and even had a layaway plan. Not a big crowd to overwhelm her like at the stores, Babe slowly went through, looking for a good deal. And as she scanned the Tv's there, to her amazement, was the television set she had owned herself. Not only was it the same style and model, but there was also the same cigarette burn on the top. The same as it was when Babe purchased it from an auction. She kept quiet and continued looking. In the music department was her stereo, which she had kept in her spare room. The stereo sat in a corner with a sold sign already attached to the big speakers. Further down was a camera and its accessories, with the unmistakable brand that was known as an antique because it was no longer being sold. Knowing it belonged to her, she continued to look in hopes of finding her other items. Around the corner was her microwave. Babe was convinced that all her things were at this pawn store.

Carefully, she pondered on what she would do and then decided not to look anymore because what she saw was enough. Immediately, she went to the salesman behind the counter and explained what she had found. When he checked his records, it was verified her items were brought in the day her house had been burglarized.

"Ever heard of Phillip Underwood?" the salesman asked.

She shook her head as if to say no.

But Phillip had already been paid, and there was nothing the salesman knew to do.

Babe left upset and surprised at the same time, thinking she should call the police station and notify them as soon as she could. At home, she dialed the police station and left a message for the detective to call her at her new number. Due to the weekend, she thought it better to wait to call the insurance adjuster.

Later that evening, Clarence called, and Babe told him what had happened at the pawnshop. Clarence could tell she was still upset over it and asked if tonight would be okay to see her. Since she was waiting for the detective to return her call, she didn't think so. Babe suggested he join her at Josie and Malcolm's the following day for dinner. Clarence had heard Babe speak of Josie and her husband, and he looked forward to meeting them. She promised she would pick him up the next day.

Even though Babe didn't think she would hear from the detective until next week, it was a good excuse, knowing she still wanted some time to herself. With the apartment half clean, she reached for a book to read while she relaxed near the fireplace. The built-in bookshelf was already being put to good use. The first book that caught her attention was the book Vince had bought her; "*101 Ways to Make Money in Photography*".

Vince was a pleasant memory, and Babe had decided he's probably involved with someone else by now. Babe had been busy with other matters in her life and never thought to visit Vince's brother and cousin, who still lived in Tulsa, and since they had only been seeing each other short of six months, it didn't seem like the relationship was strong enough to believe for more.

As she read the book, she thought of her hobby of photography. Babe really hadn't made much money in it, but she once thought it would replace the nightclub scene or add to it. Thoughts of what happened made her feel like she would probably be marked for life now, after killing that rapist. Wondering if she would ever enter a nightclub again, it all seemed so crazy, especially since she still liked to dance and party. She reflected on her life. *If anyone is to blame, it's the rapist, he was asking for trouble,* Babe thought.

Browsing through the book gave Babe ideas on how to work on the side and establish a part-time photography job; maybe a new location was perfect for a new start, she thought.

After flipping through several pages, she set the book down and allowed herself the privilege of a luxurious hot soak in the bath, and the aroma of baby-powder mist scented the condo as she absorbed the private moment for her peace and tranquility. Babe couldn't remember the last time she was able to relax without the interruption of anyone disturbing her or the fear that someone would intrude upon her. A song of thanks and praise to God was uttered from her lips as she enjoyed her newfound environment. Before she realized what she was doing, she began to feel crazy, thinking it was strange to praise God that way.

At dinner the next day, the highlight of the conversation was about Josie being pregnant. Josie and Malcolm had been trying to have another child, and it finally happened. Just the thought of a baby prompted Clarence to talk about his son, Clarence Jr. He would be two years old now, and Clarence cheered up as he bragged about how his son was holding a bottle when he was only three months old, and it had been nearly a year now since he last saw him. Josie mentioned that Markie, her firstborn, didn't seem excited about being a big brother. He had just started Head Start and didn't seem to be adjusting well with all the other children.

Clarence expressed how he missed seeing his son. Hawaii was a long way from Tulsa, and his ex-girlfriend wouldn't send him a picture.

Afterward, on the way home, Babe suggested that he call to see how Clarence Jr. was doing. Clarence thought that it would be a good idea since it was obvious how much he missed him. After settling in from the move, Babe looked forward to a productive day at work. Chaos had completely consumed her personal life during the last couple of months; her personal matters kept her too busy.

At work, Babe thought to call the detective, but decided to wait at least until noon. She moved fast to sort through the tickets and tray them up, knowing that her day would appear to be a complete waste if she didn't make up for the time on the phone.

On a normal day, her speed was fifteen trays a day, but due to the fact that the mail hadn't arrived, sometimes she would complete about twelve. Babe knew her speed was up to performance, and she always tried to help out others when she could. But when her schedule was interrupted, she would do good to get about ten trays out. Some in her group were slower than that. The older ladies were doing well to get seven trays out on a busy day; she didn't worry too much about her personal time. She felt that her speed was good enough to carry her on the bad days.

Alice was off work again; she had been having a lot of morning sickness. Most of the people in the department knew by now that Alice was expecting. Small talk about Alice was the center of attraction in the department. When Alice wasn't at work, they would pile the questions on Babe.

"Is Alice going to marry Herb?"

"Why is he doing this to her?"

Babe didn't like discussing Alice's personal business with the other employees. She considered Alice to be a friend even though they were as different as night and day. Alice enjoyed reading and waiting on Herb to be her main man; she was like a homebody. Alice looked forward to Babe telling her about the action at the nightclubs, but she would never be seen in a club, probably because she came from a small country town two hours from Tulsa. The only reason she moved to Tulsa was because the jobs were more plentiful. Herb was the first man she met and the only man she loved. Her old-fashioned ways kept her preserved, but naive. Babe didn't think Herb was faithful to Alice, but she would never tell her that.

While the group continued talking among themselves about Alice, Babe secretly prayed that Alice was doing the right thing. She lived in an efficient apartment that had the bedroom and living room together. She knew Alice didn't make a lot of money on the job, and when the baby came, it would need much more than Alice could afford on her salary.

Just as Babe looked up at the clock, the phone rang. It was for her.

"Detective Johnson," the voice said. "Did you call last weekend needing a detective?"

"Yes, sir, I called you because I had a burglary several weeks ago. Last weekend, I discovered my stolen goods at the pawn store."

As the detective listened to Babe, he recorded the information and repeated what she had said. He questioned Babe if she knew the individual that sold the items to the pawn store. Babe assured him that she didn't know the person. He told her he would get back with her after he checked into the matter.

Detective Johnson didn't call her back immediately; it was about a week after that. It was an unpleasant surprise for Babe when he told her that she would be called to testify in court at a hearing. The hearing was scheduled for Friday at nine, and today was only Monday. The guy who sold the items to the pawnshop had been apprehended, and Babe was needed to testify in court. Anxiously, she panicked as she thought of the long wait until Friday.

When she asked Detective Johnson if she had to be there, he informed her that he would subpoena her if necessary, leaving her no other choice. She agreed to cooperate.

"What's to be expected?" she wanted to know.

"They'll question your association with the assailant and whatever else they need to know pertaining to the case. Don't worry, you called me because you want to see justice done, right!"

"Of course, but I've been through hell already! What if this guy is related to the rapist?"

"We'll protect you."

Another change caused Babe to take vacation again; the entire year had been a chaos. All her vacation had been used for emergencies such as this. At work, she informed her supervisor that she needed to schedule a vacation day for Friday. When she returned to her desk, her co-worker determined by the look on her face that the news was not good. Babe explained about the upcoming trial, but her co-workers told her not to sweat it.

"Just tell it like it is," they said.

Jokingly, one supervisor called her Tiger. Yet Babe still worried if this man was related to the rapist and what would happen after she testified. Mixed emotions flooded her mind. Thoughts of defending herself flashed through her mind. Keeping the gun seemed like the logical thing to do. With the rate of crime like it was, Babe figured it was the only way to survive.

Even now she felt she would pull the trigger again if someone forcefully invaded her rights like before.

At home, just as Babe walked in and settled down, Clarence called with a tone of excitement in his voice. He told Babe that he had a chance to talk with Clarence Jr and his ex-girlfriend wanted him to come to Hawaii and spend some time with them. Babe's heart dropped as she listened to Clarence. She feared that if Clarence left for Hawaii, he would probably never return. Knowing that somehow this day would come, she knew that his heart was yearning to see his son, and if he got back with the mother, so be it, Babe thought. Anyway, it seemed like things were going from bad to worse with all the changes occurring in Babe's life. Clarence continued telling Babe that he was making plans to travel to Hawaii. As she listened to his overjoyed reaction, she decided not to tell him about the upcoming hearing.

Since he would be leaving Saturday, the day after the hearing, Babe didn't want it to keep Clarence around; she knew how excited he was about returning to Hawaii.

Babe wanted to know if Clarence was okay with a ride to the airport. It had already been planned that his cousin would take him. When Babe found out Clarence ticket was only one way, she demanded that he tell her what was really going on. Clarence gave in and told Babe that his son's mother wanted to try again at their relationship, and he felt the same way. Silence covered the airwaves, but Babe broke the silence and expressed her best wishes with them mending their relationship. It was as if Babe knew Clarence and she were going separate ways. At first, Babe wanted to make Clarence feel guilty about their breaking up, but she knew it wouldn't be fair since Clarence was secondary to all her problems and still Babe wasn't totally convinced that Clarence was the right one for her. He just came in handy for the time.

Clarence suggested they see each other before he leaves, but Babe didn't want to, knowing she had to deal with the mixed emotions of the hearing, and she didn't want to bother him with her problems, thinking somehow that might have ran him off.

"You've been a good friend that I will not forget," Babe said.

"I'm going to miss you, but I know you will be alright," Clarence said.

They hung up the phone and Babe was there thinking that she should be crying, but instead, she felt some peace in knowing that Clarence had finally realized to follow his dream, and it would be better for the both of them.

Another call interrupted Babe. It was Josie. Babe told Josie about the hearing, and Josie wanted to attend because it sounded exciting. At least that was her excuse, but Babe thought Josie was worried about her, and it was a way for her to lend some support. Babe was glad since she knew she didn't want to go alone.

It was planned that Babe would pick up Josie that morning, and they would eat lunch afterward.

Friday came faster than Babe wanted and as she prepared for the big day, she paused to pray on her knees in her bedroom. Babe considered herself a believer and talked to God in her normal way, but sometimes she didn't commit time to a strong prayer life or make sacrifices like the people in church did. She felt that if she prayed while working or walking or while preparing for sleep, it was just like any other prayer. That morning, she left early to pick up Josie; she was radiant like a light, zealous and looking forward to the day in court. Her positive attitude was the encouragement that Babe needed. Josie's enthusiasm beamed as she bragged about how courageous her little sister was, calling her a better detective than the police themselves.

Downtown Central Courthouse opened at 8:00 am. It was already full of people hanging outside of the door. Squeezing through the crowd took some tenacity that Josie displayed best, but Babe thought it would be easier just to leave and forget the whole thing, especially when she confronted the crowded room. Boldly, Josie grabbed Babe's hand and led her through the crowded section where surprisingly, they found a bench not quite full. They pressed their way through the crammed area and found a seat.

Jokingly, Babe mentioned to Josie that she was already on edge,

"I'm getting used to it, sitting on the edge of this bench."

Tension stirred as the people waited; you could hear talking and murmuring about the delayed wait. Finally, a short, stout man entered from the juror's box section. He approached the front for all to see and announced, "All stands." Simultaneously, everyone stood, and all was silent.

From behind the closed doors, the judge, a tall distinguished-looking man in a black robe, walked in and sat in the presiding judge's chair. The bailiff announced for everyone to stand before the judge came out, and after the judge sat, the Bailiff announced everyone to sit. Silence penetrated the room as the judge began to announce the cases before him.

It was near 8:30 A.M., and Babe was beginning to wonder who was first since they started late, or did they? The first case was a woman who had been caught shoplifting. The public defender pleaded with the judge for leniency, but the judge gave her five years because of her past records. Teary eyed, the woman was escorted out by a guard.

Different cases were reviewed before Babe's; Josie was in awe just looking at how the judicial system worked. Babe didn't know what to expect; she thought back to the last time she had been in court for a speeding ticket, and that was about two years ago, a memory that she didn't like after being fined $90 by the city for speeding at a rate of 90 mph.

Suddenly, a piercing voice summoned: "Valetta Juanetta Johnson," which alerted Babe that her case was up. Josie hunched Babe from her moment of daydreaming.

Nervously, she took the stand, and after being sworn in, she answered the questions as well as she knew how. The public defender asked her of her association with Philip Underwood. She denied any connection or relationship with this person. She glanced around the courtroom, trying to identify a face but recognized only Josie's. The sheriff escorted a guarded young man in prison clothing, handcuffs on his wrists, and shackles on his ankles. Babe looked him over from head to toe. Again, she was asked if she knew the person standing before her accused of the burglary, and again, she said no. As she stepped down from the stand, she looked at the frail undernourished young man, feeling sorry for him.

The worst was over, and they were allowed to leave. Josie suggested finding a McDonald's to eat at before going home. They were both hungry and looked forward to eating. As they sat at the restaurant, they struck up conversation.

"I'll bet you'll never work in a club again," Josie said while they ate.

"What's wrong with working in a club?" Babe demanded to know.

"I just thought maybe more people recognized you in a place like that," Josie said.

"As far as I'm concerned, working in a club has nothing to do with the things that have happened to me. So why should I sit around worrying about whether people are recognizing me? If anybody messes with me, they're going to get what's coming to them."

Their eyes met, and they both started laughing.

After Babe dropped Josie off at her house, she went back to the quietness of her apartment. The remote surroundings enveloped her with a sense of peace. From her bookshelf, she pulled out the book on photography, which Vince had given her, and began to read. She had the entire afternoon to herself since she didn't have to return to work.

Babe's 35mm camera was stolen during the last burglary, and a notion to replace it sounded like a good reason to go shopping.

Shopping would make the day seem like it was the vacation it was supposed to be. She had money from the insurance settlement, which was enough to buy a brand-new camera at the store. Babe tried to save money by purchasing second hand items, trying to be conservative, but they usually didn't work right. Now she felt she would finally get to own a new camera from the box, with instructions and a warranty.

At the local camera store, Babe looked at the wide choices of cameras with excitement. She purchased one with several interchangeable lenses along with some special-feature filters. It looked professional and durable, one that would last a long time. A spark of energy challenged Babe to switch to her photography hobby more.

Chapter 5

Welcomed Addition

Alice were farther along in her pregnancy, and everyone was looking forward to her expectancy. A baby shower was being planned at work. Hush-hush and whispers kept the secret in suspense while everyone bought gifts and stored them in the conference room, normally used for business meetings. Alice was somewhat petite in size, and the weight of the baby made her very pregnant as she leaned backward to walk, carrying the delicate load with ease. All the talk about Alice not being married was water under the bridge; everyone put on a good face to assure Alice that it's what made her happy that counted. She anticipated the baby more now than ever. Her ultrasound test revealed that the baby girl showed no visible signs of birth defects.

It was already planned that, for lunch, a few of the employees would take Alice on a trip to the cafeteria and return her to the conference room while everyone else prepared for the surprise. Since Alice had planned on working until she had the baby, it seemed like a good idea to have the shower during the last month the doctor predicted the arrival.

The conference room was decorated with yellow and pink bunnies; Alice knew it was a little girl, so she had already picked out a name closely related to Herb's middle name: Christine. Herb's middle name was Chris. As the door sprung open, Alice's facial expression showed that she was surprised. A seat was reserved for her near the gifts, where Babe handed her each gift to be passed around for others to see while another employee recorded who bought what. The punch and cake were desert since others had already eaten; some were eating while the shower was in progress.

After the shower, Alice called Herb to tell him about the shower and how she would need him to come prepared to help her with all the gifts. Alice was staying at Herb's apartment more now that she was almost ready to deliver, and the doctor had told Alice not to drive during the last months of her pregnancy. Herb was pleased to know they had a shower for Alice; he hadn't bought much of anything other than a baby bed. All the excitement at work left Alice feeling a little tired, so she arranged for Herb to pick her up early. Babe helped Alice gather all the gifts in a mail cart. It was near freezing outside, and Babe expressed the danger of walking on the slick pavement. Alice was well prepared with her snow boots on. The month was February, and the weather forecast predicted freezing temperatures for another week.

About the time Herb arrived, Babe had everything already loaded. All he needed to do was load the car. Herb thanked Babe and told her she didn't have to be a stranger since Alice was staying with him, extending an invitation to visit them both.

Within that week, Alice delivered a healthy eight-pound, three-ounce girl; at work, everyone feared that she would have the baby in the office. Now Alice would be off at least a month or more. It seemed like having babies was in the making.

Josie soon gave birth to another son, calling him Jerry. Josie was happy about the baby, but she wanted a daughter. Malcolm made her a promise that he would give her a daughter the next time. Josie was really busy with two kids and a husband.

Babe helped out Josie when she could; it was hard for Babe not to think about a family herself. It was Babe's plan to get serious about marriage after she reached the age of twenty-five, but it seemed like the changes that occurred in her life left her putting it off more so, and whether by chance or not, it seemed like the dates weren't serious enough for her anymore, as she could not know if she could trust a man after what had happened. Would they like her for herself, or would they only be using her or feeling sorry for her?

Babe was glad to know that she could rejoice in the families around her. She hadn't heard from Clarence since he moved to Hawaii to be closer to his son, so chances were that Clarence, and his baby momma were doing fine. It was kind of expected, Babe thought.

Nearly three months had passed before Babe heard from Vince, with the change of address and all, but the letter and souvenir she received in the mail. Puzzled her trying to figure out the small wooden vase with flora print and a stick was? It seemed like some type of depression took over her mind, and the thought of Vince reminded her of the hell she went through, causing her to forget him altogether. As she attempted to write him back it seem like Clarence impression on her left her blank and unable to write him back.

Boredom left Babe longing for involvement until a friend called; Pam called and invited her to go out with her. Babe didn't hesitate to say yes. About 10:00 pm, they headed for one of the neighborhood clubs where many older adults hung out.

Judie's Club was a more mature setting on the north side. It was busy as usual, and the security guards were on the outside checking for loafers. They entered the smoke-filled room, and the music rocked the place. The desire to party rose up within Babe. Before they could find a seat, a young man asked her to dance, and it was all the therapy she needed. Dance after dance, she seemed to make up for lost time. Later, she made her way to the seats Pam had found. And now Pam was up dancing. As Babe sat there alone, she observed two men checking her out.

She tried not to appear as if she noticed them. She picked up Pam's cigarettes, pulled one out, and lit it.

The men were whispering and staring at Babe. An alarm signal cautioned Babe. Soon one of the men approached her; he was the nicer looking one. He asked for a dance, but she kindly refused. He seemed persistent as he invited her to an after-party. When Babe told him, she wasn't able to go, he was still determined to know more about her. He asked if there was any way he could keep in touch. Their conversation seemed safe, but Babe was unsure about his motives, so she gave him a fake phone number.

He walked back to the corner where his friend stood. Babe watched him show the fake number. *Won' they be in for a surprise when they discover it's the wrong number,* she thought to herself. The other guy reminded Babe of the rapist who lay on her living room floor, and she wondered if they could be related.

When Pam returned from the dance floor, Babe started to tell her about the guy but changed her mind, thinking it might scare her and she would want to leave immediately.

Babe's suspicions began to affect her spirit as she worried inwardly how safe she was. Her expression was blank until a gentleman stepped forward, as if he knew her.

"May I have a seat?"

Babe looked up; she did recognize the young man—an associate by the name of Ronald. Babe once worked with Ronald's ex-wife, Patty. Patty's parents lived down the street from Babe, and Babe briefly dated Patty's brother, Harry. She knew Ronald had run for an office as senator of the Northeast District and was politically active as an entrepreneur of sorts.

"Considering any more political roles lately?" she asked.

"Too busy with my weekly publication. I don't have time for it anymore."

Ronald began to explain about the publication, of which he was the owner. Then he mentioned a need for a photographer. Babe listened a bit then asked him questions before suggesting herself. She explained how she loved taking pictures and had done a little freelancing, but she hadn't had the opportunity to work with a business. She offered to show Ronald her folio album, and his attitude began to radiate. She expressed hopes to supplement her income with photography. Ronald suggested that he might need her for a few daytime jobs.

Babe told him that she held a day job. "But we'll worry about that when the time comes," she said.

They exchanged numbers, and Ronald anxiously mentioned that he had a couple of assignments coming up with which he would need help.

Their mutual interest in photography had consumed the time; a waitress walked up to the table and asked if there would be any more drinks for this was the last call.

"No, thank you," Babe responded.

As they prepared to leave the club, the two men were still watching. Babe asked Ronald to walk them to the car where they talked long enough for the men to lose patience. Ronald couldn't tell Babe was just making conversation. She observed in her side-view mirror the two men get into a medium-sized beige and dark-blue 1987 Chevy Impala.

On the way home, Babe told Pam about the two men and the phony number. Pam laughed and said, "I'm glad you didn't tell me about it earlier."

The next morning, Babe was up early to do laundry. Josie called before she could get out the door. When Babe told her about the incident at the club the night before, Josie got upset, as if a big crime had been committed.

Then she apologized, saying, "I wouldn't worry about you so much if I hadn't heard that the family of the rapist wants you dead."

Unalarmed, Babe interrupted her and said, "I don't want to hear about it. If his family wants a fight, I will be forced to give them a fight, then so be it. Life is too short to live in fear. I refuse to live in fear. My gun will stay loaded, and if anyone violates my life, in all fairness, I'll have to defend myself. I don't want to hurt anyone, but in this world, if you live by the sword, you will die by the sword, and if I die then, I die, so don't worry about me."

Josie was a cosmetologist and did hair at her home. She had heard from a customer that Babe's life was in danger. Before hanging up the phone, Babe asked Josie what she would suggest. Josie could only say, "Be careful."

After hanging up the phone, the laundry still went unattended as another phone call delayed her chores—it was Ronald this time.

"I hope I didn't wake you," he said.

"Hardly, I've been up for a while."

Ronald wanted to know what Babe had planned that evening. He was scheduled to work a house party for a political party he was to cover, and Ronald wanted to know if Babe had any black-and-white films and slides, suggesting Babe accompanied him. Babe didn't expect him to call so soon, but she was ready.

That evening, Ronald picked her up at seven, and they discussed the plans and procedures. He gave her a list of instructions in order to remember whose picture she was to take. Babe didn't know the people on the list personally, but she recognized that most of them were of influential background, and she looked forward to meeting them.

The setting that evening was of formal attire, and in attendance were prominent businessmen and their wives. As they entered the two-story brick-framed Spanish Conquistador-style home, exquisitely decorated with marble and brass trinkets, Babe felt an ease of comfort when she recognized an old high school teacher displaying her artwork. Her old teacher recognized her, and they struck up conversation immediately.

After asking the teacher if it was okay to take pictures of the artwork, Babe captured the artwork on camera and marveled at how beautiful the oil paintings were and how unique the style of African heritage was. The teacher was proud of her work, you could tell by her willingness to tell Babe what each picture meant and the history. It must've been the icebreaker because, from there, the teacher introduced Babe to some of the ladies. They all identified their husbands and their businesses as well.

Ronald could see that Babe didn't need any assistance in getting to know the people. Her forward personality drew the people to her charisma. With a camera around her neck, Babe's purpose was easily identified. Babe sensed these people knew this was a way to promote their business since no one showed signs of being camera shy, and Ronald would be showing the pictures in his weekly publication.

Around her neck, she carried her camera while her shoulder-strap bag contained an assortment of interchangeable lenses.

In an attempt to change lenses, Babe sat down by a gentleman whom she knew operated a local funeral home. She introduced herself, and they began to make small talk. They discussed burials since that was his line of business; Babe mentioned that she thought cremation would be less costly. He looked at her as though she'd said something wrong. Then he quoted a Bible scripture: "From dust we're formed and to dust we will return."

"What's the difference? I believe that God will bring us back in any form or fashion," she said. "Anyway, it seems to me that cremation would be less costly."

She could tell by his puffed-up attitude that it was time to change the subject. *Naturally He Would Disagree,* she thought, *especially since he didn't offer that service.*

"Is it okay if I take a photo of you and your wife for the *Downtowner* publication before I leave?" she asked.

He consented and called his wife to join him; Babe quickly took the photo and thanked them both before leaving to meet the rest of the lively group.

Everyone mingled with one another as an introduction and speech was being expressed by the host. He reminded them why they were all there, encouraging them to vote and let their voices be heard, making a difference in the community. Briefly he introduced some of the key people, along with acknowledging Ronald and his assistant. With a smile on his face, he looked at Babe.

He sure knows how to make a person feel as if they belong, Babe thought.

The two-story house was full of people on both levels. The refreshments were downstairs level. An urge to quench her thirst led Babe to the refreshments table before making her way upstairs. Timing was well enough to meet the homeowner and the host of the party, an attorney with an established law firm. Babe commended him on the collection of certificates and degrees that decorated his wall.

He is a humble man, Babe thought when he took no less credit than to give God the Glory. Maybe he thought Babe was religious since she had her cross around her neck; he didn't know it was Babe's custom by now.

Before long, Babe had met everyone downstairs; she followed the spiral staircase upstairs. There she found Ronald with several men, watching a football game on TV.

"How did it go downstairs?" he asked.

"No one's discussing the election," she mentioned. "I got plenty of pictures and made notes of all the names as well."

Ronald explained that this meeting was simply a get-acquainted party; he suggested that she photograph a few of the men in the corner, who should be acknowledged.

They were finished after taking about two rolls of film. As the people gathered their belongings, the crowd began to diminish. It was late when Ronald and Babe left. They both talked about what a good group of people it was, not like the nightclubs Babe mentioned. She told Ronald about a fashion show she photographed at the Celebrity Nightclub; the same night the club had sponsored a group that had performed at the local pavilion center and had a sellout crowd—a walltowall of people with the commotion of chaos. Ronald assured Babe his assignments were low-key with low risks involved. Just as he said that Babe thought he was trying to say something about the justifiable homicide.

Thinking to herself, Babe thought it wouldn't be fair to withhold it from Ronald, especially if her working with him would put him at risk of endangering his life since Josie had already warned Babe what people were saying. Just when conversation was at a highpoint, Babe knew that she would have to tell Ronald. She waited until he expressed his last sentence about the party. Then she asked him if he heard about the rapist that was killed by his victim. Ronald tried to appear as if he didn't know what she was talking about. Babe admitted to what happened and asked Ronald if it would make a difference in what they were doing. He then acknowledged hearing about it and applauded her for her bravery, expressing that it would be an honor to work with her instead of a risk.

Relief overwhelmed Babe as she thought, how many people have to talk about the justifiable homicide? Why can't they bury it like the rapist?

It was late when they finally drove up to Babe's condo. Ronald expressed that it was considerate of her to tell him, even though Babe didn't seem to worry about her life. She knew that she didn't want to endanger anyone on her behalf. Babe didn't invite Ronald in; she told him to call her, and she would let him know when the pictures would be ready. The film developer wasn't open that Sunday, and it would be over the weekend before dropping them off. Babe thought it would be at least next week.

Ronald called earlier instead of the following week. He had other things on his mind. The next day being Sunday was a mission for Ronald to invite Babe to attend church with him. He called Babe early with an open invitation for church with him. Babe vaguely remembered he had mentioned that he was Catholic the night before.

"I'm not interested," Babe said.

Ronald didn't want to take no for an answer as he tried to bring a stronger conviction on her about not attending church. Babe didn't know how to respond without reverencing God. For some reason, Babe knew that she wasn't interested in the Catholic faith, but yet it seemed like she didn't follow any faith other than her own. Ronald preached a sermon about assembling oneself with other believers, and Babe didn't argue with him; she only agreed to think about it.

Within minutes of talking to Ronald, Babe felt a surge of anger as she thought that Ronald would be a normal friend whom she could learn from. She didn't feel attracted to Ronald and didn't want to hurt his feelings. Another puzzling fact was that she began to realize that she didn't feel drawn into the Catholic church, regardless of whether she liked Ronald as a special friend or not.

Before ending the conversation with Ronald, Babe decided to level with him and be honest about her feelings. She told Ronald that she would seek out her own soul's salvation, and she wasn't particularly interested in attending a Catholic church; furthermore, she looked at Ronald as a friend and business associate and didn't want him to be misled.

He seemed to understand her refusal, but her decision weighed heavily on her heart. She thought about the different denominations. How can they all be the same with different traditions and rituals? Then she convinced herself that she had Jesus in her heart, and as soon as she was settled in her ways, she would find a church that suited her.

That week, Babe picked up the pictures. She was pleased with how well they turned out. She couldn't wait to tell Ronald. His anticipation was high as well because the phone was ringing when she arrived at her apartment door.

When she told him how well they looked, he said,

"Say no more. I'll be right over."

They looked over the pictures, and both marveled over the clarity and distinctive focus they showed. Ronald paid her for the work and the pictures and thanked her, reaching to embrace her in a sensual way, but she stepped back, trying to block his move.

"Does this mean you don't want to see me anymore?" he asked.

"If there's a photography job, I'd love to help, but I don't want the relationship to become too personal."

When he left, Babe could tell he was hurt. She was sorry he was hurt, but she knew he would be misled if she didn't make things clear to him. When he failed to contact her for further assignments, she realized he had taken it personally.

Babe decided not to worry about things like Ronald, knowing that friends come and go.

Chapter 6

Moving Didn't Matter

It was just a matter of time before the IUD Babe had inserted right after her abortion began to cause her a few medical problems. Babe had to have it surgically removed because it should have been removed after years; however, ten years had already passed, and it created some problems. After it was surgically removed, the doctor told Babe that she wouldn't be able to have any children. Babe was upset at first, but after she thought about it, she realized that she didn't have to worry about birth control anymore. After the doctor removed it surgically, she was able to return to work and felt no side-effects afterward. Babe was glad that she had insurance to take care of everything.

Several years had passed, and Babe had gone through two different sets of tenants, and she was getting tired of living in apartments. Babe almost missed her home, but she thought about the problems, and she began to think of how she could afford a better home closer to family.

Babe had equity in the rented home, and she thought she would consult with a real estate agent about refinancing the house which would allow Babe a chance to move back into a house. She was beginning to think apartments were a waste of money—no room to grow in.

When Babe called up an old church member that sold homes, he told Babe that it would be a good idea since she had the mortgage on the home for several years now. Mr. Langford was instrumental in helping Babe go through the refinancing, and when it was done, he knew that she would use him to purchase another home.

The refinancing went off perfect on a second mortgage. When the loan officer presented Babe with a check for $12,000, she wanted to sign the papers and kiss everyone there, but she calmed herself so she could go over the details of the new mortgage note. The rental house payment wasn't as much as the monthly rent coming in, so she would have no problem meeting that obligation.

Babe left quickly to notify Mr. Langford. He was pleased and said she would be more qualified for a better house now. They agreed and began looking as soon as possible. Mr. Langford's persistence wore Babe out; she could tell Mr. Langford wanted her to hurry with a decision, but Babe didn't see any homes she liked.

Eventually, when she did find one that she liked, it had an "As is" sign on it. The appearance of the house attracted Babe, and she was willing to take a chance, so she put $1,500 down as a security deposit. Mr. Langford warned her that since it was "As is," if the loan company didn't approve the loan, the agency could keep her deposit. But Babe felt sure she would be approved since one mortgage company had already approved a second mortgage.

Finding a source to finance the house was the next project. She checked with the bank located in the same office building where she worked. When she was informed that she had been rejected because of the state of the house, she panicked. Quickly, Babe left work early to apply with another bank.

After a couple of days, the second bank notified her that she was again denied financing for the house. Her hopes began to diminish; she didn't understand. The house had everything she wanted: three bedrooms, two-car garage, large combo living room with built-in appliances, a sliding patio door, central heating and air-conditioning, and bars already on the windows. It was the perfect house, priced at $13,000 below the appraised value. It was a good deal. Babe was disappointed when she didn't get the loan, and now she was concerned about the deposit as well.

Babe called Mr. Langford and explained that the house couldn't be financed. He was disappointed because he knew she might not get her money back. The clause in the contract clearly stated it. Mr. Langford did taxes at the end of the year and suggested Babe to claim it as a loss on her income tax. When he saw that advice wasn't comforting, he suggested talking to the director of government housing development. That sounded like a better idea.

"Tomorrow, I'll let you know when he'll see you," Mr. Langford told her.

The next day, Mr. Langford had bad news. "Mr. Jones, the director, is a firm man who honors only what's in the contract."

But Babe wasn't ready to give up so soon; she wanted to speak to Mr. Jones herself. So, she called and made an appointment with Mr. Jones herself. Babe didn't know what she was going to say, but she knew she had to talk to him. She pictured him as a big guy who never smiled, but to her surprise, he was a short, stocky man who wasn't that difficult to talk with.

Babe explained how she really wanted the house, but that the financing sources just didn't come through. She explained that the first house she bought was a government home. She is just trying to make small talk, hoping Mr. Jones would restore her faith in the system. She asked Mr. Jones if he would suggest a way to get the house financed. He informed her it was too late for that particular house because a couple had already gotten it financed and was preparing to move in.

"However," Mr. Jones went on, "we do have a special selection of houses at a special interest rate. They haven't been advertised on the new list yet. You can have the first choice."

He showed her the special payment plan and then showed her his personal list of homes for sale and advised her to have a real estate broker notify him when she came to a decision.

Babe walked out of his office; she felt she had a ray of hope and immediately called Mr. Langford. There were only twelve houses on the list, and she had a week to make up her mind.

They went through the list fast because none of the houses were as nice as the one Babe really wanted. Mr. Langford was getting annoyed with her response; she was in a quandary. Everyone had been so nice to help her, but she was getting weary. Mr. Langford told her they would let her select new carpeting, and they would winterize the house before she moved in, which was encouraging to know.

It wasn't long before Babe selected a house just a couple of miles from Josie's home.

Within a month, Babe had moved in. Her first visitor was Josie. She brought a housewarming present and toured the house.

"Don't bother me now," she teased, "just because we live a few miles apart."

"Don't worry," Babe responded. "Knowing you and those kids, I'll have to pretend like I'm not home half the time."

Josie praised her accomplishments, but Babe gave all the glory to God. Since Josie was of the Jehovah's Witness belief, she didn't comment. Babe sensed she must have said something wrong because Josie left soon after.

Employment at work was flourishing. Babe had a new position that allowed overtime, which kept her from seeking part-time work. The people in the department seemed nice. On a few occasions, Babe would find herself joining another department on the same floor for lunch. One girl had been an acquaintance with Babe since her teen years; they lived in the same neighborhood. While sharing with a couple of ladies during lunch, Babe discussed with them that she had worked for another oil company. One employee asked if she knew her sister when she worked at the other oil company. When she mentioned her name, Babe did remember. Her sister had been a devout Christian, whom Babe remembered was always praising the Lord. Babe had thought she was different, and then she learned of her tragic death. She was found dead, locked in the trunk of her car. That's when Babe's old neighborhood friend turned the conversation to Babe and asked about the time, she killed that man.

Caught a little off guard, Babe told Cherry, "I don't want to talk about it, you can read the paper."

Silence covered the air as Babe gathered her things to leave and politely told the group it was time for her to return to work. Cherry didn't seem to be upset with Babe's response as she expressed to Babe to join them another time.

When Babe started back to work, she felt bad about the cold response she had given her. But she really didn't want to talk about it, especially not in front of a group. So many people had falsely accused her of wrongdoing—people didn't know the whole story. She didn't want any more rumors to start.

She hated that the killing ever happened. She wanted to forget the whole thing, but everywhere she went, someone identified her with the incident. Through her tears, she told herself that she did what she had to do. Even in the Bible there were men of God who had to fight for their rights.

Free from working the extra jobs left Babe seeking something else to do. Time was beginning to mature Babe, and she didn't want to party as much, not to mention that most of her friends had started drifting off. Pam moved to Texas, and Alice returned to her hometown to go back to school after she had her second child.

On the way home from work one day, Babe went the long way, and as she crossed the lights a mile away from home, the little church on the corner suddenly caught Babe's attention. Then she remembered Mary, a high school classmate who had invited her to the church long ago, when Babe still enjoyed partying.

It seemed like Babe could remember it as if it were yesterday when she called Mary, seeking someone to party with her that night. All her other friends and associates were out of pocket. Mary was quick to remember that night after graduation, when Babe and a few of her friends were together for the last time, and now they're either all married or divorced.

Everyone wanted to do something exciting, like find a party, but Babe wanted to find a church and go to a revival. Mary had since settled down and became a mother and wife and was trying to recruit souls for the kingdom of God. As Babe listened, Mary had been praying for Babe ever since she switched lifestyle because she knew Babe sounded like she had known God and would always know him. But as time passed on, the church didn't make any lasting impact on Babe. Babe realized the several brushes with death were interventions from God that saved her life.

Suddenly, Babe realized as she passed that little church on that corner that maybe God was trying to save her for his will after all. By the time Babe turned in her driveway, she thought perhaps she could call up Mary and find out more about that little church on the corner. Of course, Mary was glad to hear from Babe since she was still in the business of recruiting souls.

She told Babe that they had a new believers' group Babe should attend on Wednesday. It was Friday, and after hanging up, Babe thought she would try to attend next week and possibly Sunday.

That weekend, things took a turn when Pam came in from Dallas and called Babe up to party. It wasn't every day that Babe heard from Pam, and she was glad to hear from her.

Pam's sister, Andrea, joined them at the nightclub that night along with an ex-neighbor. With everyone together, it seemed like old times. Babe thought about the days when they all lived in the same neighborhood. Pam stayed across the street from Babe with a neighbor that she almost married. Diane stayed a couple of doors down, and Andrea lived around the corner. The gathering was like a reunion.

At the nightclub that evening, Babe's half-brother, Sonny, was there. It had been a long time since she had seen him. Sonny drove a semi-truck and traveled a lot. After filling him in on the family business, he shared with Babe some of the adventures in long-distance driving. Sonny loved to party when he was in town, and he knew a number of people. At the table, a gentleman came up and asked if he could sit with them. Babe was curious about him.

Sonny introduced his friend as Curt. Curt offered to buy everyone a drink; he seemed like a flirt. He was quick to let her know he was like family.

The body heat from the dancing began to warm up the club. Sonny and Curt went out for a breath of fresh air. This gave Babe an opportunity to ask Pam about Curt since they're both from the same rural town.

Pam said simply, "He hung out with my older brother. I'm not sure what he's like."

When they returned, Curt's suave personality was more charming than before. He had Babe's curiosity aroused. While Curt danced, Babe questioned Sonny about him.

Sonny's response was, "He was just a good ole homeboy back when we were growing up, I haven't seen him in a while, and I don't guess he changed."

Curt was persistent in showing an interest in Babe, and she wondered if there could be anything to him. In a conversation, he told her he was a licensed welder. *At Least The Potentials Are There,* Babe thought, since it made a difference to her whether a guy had a job or not. Before Curt left, he must've passed the test, for Babe gave him her number.

Babe decided that before the girls left, she would invite them over for dinner since they hadn't seen Babe's new place. At dinner, Pam warned Babe that Curt and her brother were in the fast life.

Babe told her not to worry. "I've reached the conclusion that I'm not falling for anyone until Mr. Right comes along."

It wasn't long before Curt did call, and Babe found herself putting him off. She didn't feel like being bothered with anyone, and he was no exception. When he finally caught her in a good mood, they talked on the phone. Curt invited Babe to the movies, and she accepted, thinking there can be no harm in it. The movie was great, and the fact that Curt was a jack-of-all-trades left Babe thinking of greater potentials. Babe didn't want to take things too fast because she didn't know if he was serious or just wanted to play games.

Babe had successfully leased her house out for three years. It didn't surprise her to run into complications. The tenant leased through a government agency, which inspected periodically. Babe was notified that she needed to make some repairs before it would pass inspection. Replacing the kitchen and bathroom tiles wasn't an easy job, but she figured she could save money if she did it herself. Babe called Josie and asked her to help; Babe had helped her do her kitchen, so she was ready for the challenge. Josie was preoccupied, so she purchased all the supplies and began the job herself.

Curt would call from time to time, but since she couldn't get Josie to help her out with the floors, Curt came to the rescue. When Babe discussed her plans to lay tiles in the rented house, he asked if he could help. Babe was more than grateful to accept his help.

Thanks to Curt, the tiles were properly installed. Looking at the size of the job, she couldn't have done it alone. While observing the outside of the house, she could tell it was time for a paint job, when Curt called again. Babe offered to pay him if he would help paint. He wasn't excited about the paint job, but after Babe offered to cook dinner for a week, he had a change of heart.

They started immediately since there was a deadline to meet or the government would delay the rent or terminate the lease. The house needed to be sanded in most of the areas before they got started. After they got started, they had a pretty good time since they started early that morning. By evening, it was all over.

Curt's help was really appreciated. Babe paid him what she agreed to pay him. Since they both painted the house together, he didn't complain about the arrangement. He liked her company more than anything.

Time brought out a different side to Curt, and Babe grew to like him more. They began to spend more time together; she never needed to call him, but one day, when she did, a lady answered. Babe thought she had the wrong number until she verified that Curt did live there but wasn't home. The lady took Babe's name and said she would have Curt call her.

Somewhat surprised that a woman would be occupying Curt's home since he had not told Babe about her, Babe couldn't help but wonder if something was going on between them. But she decided not to judge too fast. After all, she had a male roommate once, and the situation was strictly platonic.

That evening, Curt phoned, and Babe asked him about the woman. He said she had been put out of her apartment and needed a place to stay. Babe believed him and was glad that he offered to help someone in need. But when Babe continued to call him, the woman's voice changed from pleasant to not-so-pleasant. Thinking it was only her imagination, Babe tried to overlook the situation.

Curt eventually had to move his lady friend out since she wasn't very friendly to Babe when she called. That gave them more private time to talk about the future. Curt began to talk about having children, and Babe's hopes turned to gloom when she remembered complications from the contraceptive device that damaged her female organs and what the doctor told her. She didn't want to mislead Curt, so she told him what the doctor had told her when he took the device out. Curt's humor was always uplifting as he joked about what fun it would be in trying, but when she suggested adoption to him, he hunched his shoulders. Babe could tell he wasn't thrilled with the idea.

When Babe wasn't with Curt, she watched Josie's children. Now Josie has three children. Malcolm made good on his promise to give Josie a daughter, but all of a sudden, Josie had a busy schedule, and Babe didn't understand why. Josie had no job, so Babe couldn't understand what was keeping her busy. Babe didn't mind keeping her two smallest children because they kept her motivated. Jerry and Sharon were mischievous and always had something going on. They were friends with other kids in the neighborhood, and when they got on Babe's nerves, she would send them next door to play.

Slowing down from her busy schedule gave her time to consider going to that church Mary attended. Babe called Mary and told her to look for her; she would finally be attending the new believers' class.

The first night of Bible study, Babe understood how blessed she was to have lived through the things she did, and she hoped that someday she would be able to pay God back for his kindness to her. She was enlightened to see some familiar faces stand to share their testimony. An old neighbor gave his testimony about how he came to Christ and had made a change for the good.

Anxiously, Babe waited to tell Curt about church that evening. When he called, Babe told him about the Bible study;

he wanted to know what she had learned. Babe told him about the testimonies that went forth, and since it was the first night, they discussed the curriculum that had to be ordered, but several testimonies she heard were uplifting as they gave all the glory to God.

Curt changed the subject and asked Babe to go to a party with him over the weekend. That weekend, they went to the party, and the party lasted so long that Babe overslept and wasn't able to make it to church that Sunday. She recalled waking up in time but dreaded getting up for that purpose.

Finally, a visit from Josie woke Babe up. To her surprise, she had a few things for her—a bottle of cologne and a few brass trinkets that someone had given her. When Babe asked why she was giving them to her, she claimed that she owned the same things. Babe went on to explain about the church she had attended and her plans to attend church that morning but slept too late.

After a pause, Babe couldn't resist asking Josie about Kingdom Hall, a church she once attended. She told Babe they stopped going because her brother-in-law was asked to remove his membership after he and his wife divorced.

"It seems something else might have been done instead of such harsh punishment," Babe stated.

Josie had married into that denomination and just went along with her husband most of the time. Babe could remember the zeal she first had when her marriage was new. She was full of energy, going door-to-door witnessing for Jehovah's Witnesses. It was like you couldn't help but see the good in the people. Babe really did admire them, and she knew it took more than a notion to go door-to-door. Having the door slammed in your face had to be insulting, but they continued to work for the Lord.

It really hit a sore spot when Josie switched her faith to Jehovah's Witnesses since the family was raised Baptist, but it seemed like they weren't much Baptist anyway. For some reason, Babe didn't know enough about the Jehovah's Witnesses faith, but because they were trying to lift up the name of the Lord in some way or another, Babe just thought they should be respected and dealt with in a more diplomatic way.

Chapter 7

One Thing Led to Another

Something was going awry, and it wasn't clear what it was. Babe's attendance at the little church didn't seem to make a difference with Curt or Josie since they were her most regular visitors.

One evening, Josie stopped by and convinced Babe to go with her over to a friend's house. At her friend's house, Josie introduced Babe to Joyce, who looked as if she had just crawled out of bed. Joyce showed them to her bedroom, where she opened her closet. This closet was like nothing she'd ever seen. It was a shopper's paradise. New garments hung on the rack with the tags still attached, boxes of shoes galore, and in another corner were a selection of brass trinkets and bottles of cologne and perfume.

Josie insisted that Babe select a dress and a bottle of perfume. When Babe asked how much it would cost her, Josie said, "It's on me. I wanted to pay you for all the times you kept my kids."

Babe didn't think twice when she said that. The selection was vast; it took her a few minutes to choose the dress she wanted. Finally, she found a silk dress—which was a lavender floral-print fully lined dress. The original price tag said $115. Babe asked Josie if this one was okay. Josie nodded then reminded her to choose a bottle of perfume as well. Perfume was always a hit with Babe, and she knew them well, it only took a minute to select Channel 21, a fragrance that she hadn't owned, but she knew Chanel anything was a good fragrance.

Joyce sacked up everything as if they were in a store. When they left, Babe asked Josie what that was all about.

"Joyce is a booster," Josie said. "She does that for a living."

"What's a booster?" Babe asked.

"A shoplifter."

"You mean these things are stolen?"

Sure enough, that was exactly what she meant.

Josie was slow in responding, but then explained that her husband, Malcolm, did business with her. Malcolm was always in some kind of a business deal, but she couldn't imagine what she meant. Malcolm had a horse he had bought and was involved in gambling at the horse races, but Malcolm had gotten so bad about gambling that he couldn't hold a conversation without betting you something.

That evening, when Curt visited, Babe showed him the new dress and told him about Joyce. When Curt confessed that he knew Joyce, Babe was dumbfounded.

"When I used to sell drugs, Joyce would exchange stolen goods for the drugs," Curt explained.

Curt had never elaborated on that part of his past, but since Babe accepted Curt for who he was and not for what he had done in the past, she decided not to investigate the situation.

Josie and Curt soon met and found out they knew most of the same people. Babe couldn't help but wonder what really was going on. It wasn't long before Curt and Malcolm met, and since they hit it off so well, plans were made to attend the horse race together.

The four of them coupled off and decided to take a trip to the horse races. Malcolm owned a horse and had him in training. That was another one of his ideas for making money.

Afterward, Malcolm and Curt began to run together, and it seemed like more than a coincidence that they hit it off so fast. It seemed like Babe and Josie were the closest in the family now since they lived so close, and for some reason, Josie was slowly building a wall against Malcolm's family. Babe remembered how close Josie used to be with Malcolm's family, and she couldn't figure it out, maybe because they were all Jehovah's Witnesses and the disappointment of Malcolm's brother being banned from the church.

Josie and Malcolm's fifteenth-year anniversary were coming up, and Babe thought perhaps she would want her to keep the children, but instead, Josie asked Babe to hold a small reception.

A few appetizers and drinks drew the people that Josie had casually invited—nothing big since Babe was caught off guard with the very request. Her small house wasn't quite the site for a nice formal gathering, but then since your home is your palace, Babe thought the people that came would be comfortable. And all of a sudden, Babe was the ear that Josie confided in.

Josie stopped by for regular visits. Babe sensed that something was on her mind, but she wouldn't open up.

One evening, Josie picked up her children from Babe's house and sat down to talk. While Jerry and Sharon were still at the neighbor's, she asked if Babe had used cocaine. Out of the blue, the question was asked. Babe started to say never but thought about the party she went to long ago with Pam, where cocaine was used in a pipe and was smoked.

"Did you like it?" she asked.

"I don't remember any special effects at that time and didn't see any need in fighting over it, that's how the party ends."

Josie brought out a little white paper that looked like a gum wrapper. Gently she opened the paper, displaying the sparkling white powder.

"What's that?" Babe asked.

"Top-of-the-line cocaine," Josie said. With a small straw in one hand, she leaned forward to sniff a line in her nose. "Try it," she urged.

Babe reached over to do the same and blew cocaine all over the table.

Josie panicked. "Don't you know how to sniff?" she demanded.

"Let me try again." This time it wasn't so bad.

Babe sniffed it up her nose, and within minutes, she began to feel a tingling sensation inside her body, and her mind shifted into a faster gear.

They sat there talking about cocaine and how it was supposed to be a recreational drug. She said it increased a person's thinking ability. "Lots of people use it to study with." she explained.

Babe wasn't sure about all of that, but she figured it was expensive. Babe tried to get Josie to tell her where she had gotten the stuff, but she told her she'd rather not say.

After the paper containing the white crystal powder was empty. Josie pulled out another one, but she still wouldn't reveal her secret.

That thin line of cocaine gave Babe such a lift, she cleaned house, constantly looking out the window, making sure the children didn't walk in to see this while Josie sat there talking. "Does this stuff always affect people this way?"

"Usually it does," Josie said, "but it affects people differently, and some use it differently."

Eventually, Josie went across the street to pick up the kids. Sharon and Jerry would get so involved in playing that they would forget they had to go home. After Josie left, Babe found herself wanting more of the white powder until she realized that's how people get hooked on the stuff. *Maybe it wouldn't be so questionable if it was used in moderation,* she thought.

Josie had no restrictions on visiting after that, and she always had some white powder with her. This wasn't like Josie. She didn't smoke cigarettes, and now she was smoking secretly behind Malcolm's back.

One evening after work, Babe wanted to go home and rest, but the moment she lay down, Josie stopped by. She had some errands to run and was hoping Babe would go with her. Babe could tell Josie wasn't going to leave, so she grabbed her things to go.

It must have taken about forty-five minutes before they reached the destination. They passed several road signs indicating that they were no longer in town. While Josie was driving, she noticed Babe nodding, so she passed over a package of her stash. After taking a sniff, Babe told her they should call this stuff eye-opener. She stayed alert after that.

Outside of Tulsa City limits and into Glen Arrow, a new housing edition, Josie pulled into the driveway of a nice two-story house. When the car came to a stop, Babe quickly asked, "Who lives here?"

"You don't know them," was all she said.

Excitedly, a man answered the door and showed them in. It was obvious he was expecting them. The house was in disarray. At the dining room table, Josie brought out a small, clear plastic package with white powder, and he brought out a sack for exchange. His sack was full of all types of medicine. He also gave Josie some money to even things out. After the exchange was made, they left.

It was apparent that Josie was much deeper than Babe knew. At last, she told her that Malcolm had been getting drugs from a dealer who fronts it to him after it's sold, and Malcolm gets more drugs.

Josie was surprised that Babe didn't know since Malcolm and Curt had been working together, and then she realized why their association was so close.

Back at the house, they talked about it some more as they both snorted from her personal package.

"How much longer do you and Malcolm plan to be involved in this mess?" Babe asked.

Josie simply hunched her shoulders as if to say, "I don't know."

Malcolm had dreamed of opening his own feed store and becoming self-employed.

After seeing Josie off that night, Babe lay in bed, wondering if it was a sin to use cocaine. She tried to reason with herself that it was probably all right if used in moderation. Then she realized it was a sin to use money for that when there were many needy and hurting people in the world who could use a meal or a place to lay their head. Babe's conclusions left her justifying that only the elite, who were rolling in money, could afford to use cocaine.

Babe knew that Curt used cocaine because Malcolm and Josie made it so available, but she didn't know Malcolm was running Curt. When she questioned Curt about his involvement, he admitted that he helped Malcolm at times. He always seemed to keep drugs after that. Babe began to enjoy it more and never gave a thought to what it could lead to. However, she had her limits. Using cocaine was for pleasure until they began to question her about going in on a deal; that's when she said no. Josie had exposed her to freebies, and it was nothing for her to bring a package of cocaine. But that was no reason for Babe to make a career out of it.

As time went by, Babe saw the drastic change the white powder was making in everyone's lives. She began to look forward to running errands with Josie, knowing there was a bonus to appreciate afterward. Curt wanted to lease out his house in order to change locations, and they agreed that if he moved in with Babe, they could split the bills. Since Josie and Malcolm had been in and out of the house, Babe began to feel uncomfortable being alone.

Curt's presence didn't matter much after he moved in. He stayed out half the night, or all night, working with Malcolm. When he did come home, he would start on drugs himself, turning Babe on and starting a desire that only left after consuming valium, which would put her to sleep. The habit and craving for drugs grew worse. Babe was beginning to check herself; she knew she didn't like what she was seeing, and truly she was regretting it. A notice was made that it wasn't the rich buying cocaine; a big percent of their customers were oppressed welfare recipients.

At times, Babe would cry herself to sleep, praying to God that he would stop her from using drugs, yet she still did not want to admit that it was a real problem to Josie since it was their career.

While at home one evening, Babe answered the door, and it was Josie. She was trying to catch her breath and calm down.

"What's the matter with you?" Babe asked her.

She paused to drink her beer then told her story. She had attempted to make a delivery when the people said they needed to go to the store to get change. Instead of getting change, they were going to rob the store. They were frightened away when the police pulled up. Josie was in the car with them.

"I didn't even know they had a gun until we drove away," she said.

"That ought to be enough to make you want to leave the stuff alone," Babe told her.

Josie began to confide in Babe since she was her only friend; she told her that she loved her, but Babe had to interrupt Josie and tell her that she's going to need to face reality about the drug scene. She also told her it would be better if she and Malcolm would leave the drugs alone.

Josie insisted, however, that Malcolm was determined to make money in this and was now considering quitting his job. Babe shuddered as she thought of the new car they had recently purchased.

"Josie, why don't you get a full-time job and let him do drugs if he has to?" Babe suggested. Since Josie had never been anything but a housewife, with the exception of a few part-time jobs, she wasn't sure anyone would even hire her.

But the suggestion was taken. Together they scanned the classified ads each day, and Babe would call her from work to get her motivated. Sometimes the phone would ring twenty times before she finally answered it.

Josie's search for a job was difficult because she was looking for good pay. She had been deluded by the vast opportunities the drugs afforded her. She was able to exchange drugs for food, clothes and all sorts of miscellaneous items, which left her feeling secure.

Joyce supplied her with clothes for her children regularly. Joyce became so familiar with Babe she didn't think twice to stop by the place if she was looking for Josie. Josie was at the house so much her customers would stop by as well.

Curt stayed gone half the time and Babe found herself turning to drugs more. Pleasure was found in doing cocaine without him; it seemed more economical, and she didn't have friends, nor did she want any because when people found out she was related to a drug dealer, it became the focal point for the friendship—to have a better connection.

Babe discovered there weren't too many people you could trust. Josie warned her that people came to her because they were sisters, and she gave her discounts. She was right! Her customers were exceptionally nice and did everything they could to be friendly. But Babe had to keep a wall up, or they would try to use her.

As long as Babe continued to make it to work, she felt she didn't have a habit to worry about. But soon she wanted more than Josie could give. Withdrawals from her accounts left concerned that she was more deeply involved than she realized.

Curt was paying for half the expenses, which left her ahead in that area, but then Babe used that money toward drugs. Curt was upset when he learned what she was doing. He insisted that she invest that money instead of blowing it off so she could make a profit and still spend on her habit. Babe did try Curt's suggestion, but soon found she was losing money with him because he controlled everything, and she couldn't trust him. Josie then told Babe how Curt had worked with Malcolm on a deal and wasted the drugs he should have made money with. Strife developed in their relationship, and Josie began to warn Babe against Curt.

One morning, Babe was awakened by the phone. It was Josie. They talked about how the drug dealing was becoming even more frightening.

"If anything happens to me, Babe, would you keep the children?"

Babe was frightened, but she didn't hesitate to say yes. Josie was bitter and broke; she was doing good to keep the bills paid, and she was fed up with all the problems she was having with Malcolm and his family.

After their conversation on the phone, Babe fell to her knees and prayed that nothing would happen to her beloved sister.

Returning to that little church was the last thing on Babe's mind since she became involved with drugs and Curt. She just couldn't feel right about going to church.

Upon visiting another sister, Candi, whose husband smoked marijuana and purchased it from Malcolm, Candi noticed the change in Josie also and questioned Babe. She knew they were involved in drugs. Candi and her family didn't go to church; Babe thought their prayers would get through faster than hers. She asked her to pray for them.

One Saturday morning, Babe had slept late but was soon awakened to the phone ringing. It was Markie, Josie's oldest son, asking if she knew where his parents were. They hadn't come home last night, and he thought perhaps they were at Babe's house. Markie said they had no breakfast. Concerned and worried, Babe hurried over to see what she could do.

On the way, she couldn't help but remember what Josie said about keeping the kids if anything happened to her. Even though she had told her she would, she wondered if she could actually afford to do it. When Babe got there, Josie and Malcolm had just walked in. They were tired; they went right to bed while the kids and Babe went out for breakfast.

Keeping the kids all day and that night gave Josie and Malcolm some time to rest. When Josie picked them up, Babe could tell she was upset, but she wouldn't tell Babe why.

Somehow Babe could tell they'd been fighting. From the different things Josie had told Babe, she knew Malcolm had begun to act like his dope-dealer friend who felt he had to hit a woman to prove he's a man.

Josie had a way of hiding most of the problems about her marriage. She knew Babe would be honest and tell her how she felt, and Josie wouldn't be able to take anything said against Malcolm. Once, Babe suggested that Josie separate until their lives were straightened out. Josie didn't want to hear it, and they nearly got into an argument over it.

Trying not to say anything against Malcolm was hard, especially when Josie spoke out against Curt. It didn't bother Babe because she wasn't in love with Curt, and he could be out of her life without a second thought. But it wasn't that easy for Josie.

Christmas was just around the corner. It wasn't planned; something just happened, and the entire family planned a gathering. James from Los Angeles had come to town with some friends and called Josie to pick him up at a nearby town. Two other brothers from Dallas came in unexpectedly. It was only a couple of days before Christmas, and all Babe's shopping was done. She felt she had accomplished a great feat.

Josie's family didn't celebrate Christmas, so Babe wouldn't wrap their gifts. When Josie stopped by and saw all the wrappings for the other gifts, she then requested that Babe wrap her family gifts this time. Babe did just that.

Dinner was at Papa's house and then a small reunion at Josie's afterward. Papa was glad to have them all together. They were not as close as other families, but they tried to make the best of the occasion. At Josie's house, everyone ate more and played games.

The Christmas spirit and other spirits were lively that night as they drank and played card games. The children tore open their gifts and thanked Babe for everything. It was surely a delight to see the children overwhelmed with excitement in their eyes. It was all new to them to be like the other kids and receive wrapped gifts at Christmas time.

While the men were all playing cards with old neighborhood friends, Josie and Babe both observed how thin and frail their older brother James was. He coughed a lot.

Some were concerned that he smoked too much. Babe went out and purchased some cough syrup for him.

While the guys played cards, Josie and Babe talked. Josie mentioned how rare it was for a family to get together as they had.

"I've heard there's usually a death afterward," she said.

After Christmas, things returned to the same lifestyle. The New Year had Babe thinking about resolutions and new beginnings; she knew she had kidded herself about cocaine far too long. Even though she enjoyed it, she knew it was taking a toll on her life as well as others around her. Too many problems had developed because of it, and the only way to a better life would be to leave it behind.

Then Josie called and told Babe Malcolm had quit his job. Babe knew they talked about it, but now that he did, she knew this meant trouble. Now they would have to rely solely on selling cocaine on a regular basis. Before long, their habits were as bad as their customers.

Their condition worsened as everyone else's did, and when they ran out of cocaine, they desperately searched for a fix, calling around to buy drugs for themselves. It got to a point where Babe didn't want to be with Josie. And since Josie knew how paranoid Babe was, she didn't bother Babe as much.

Curt talked about marriage and tried to convince Babe that it would work, but Babe was doubtful, knowing she didn't love him. Babe tried to convince herself that she could learn to love him. He purchased a ring, but they didn't set a date. There were too many things that needed to be resolved first. Babe was tired of his involvement with drugs and told him that their relationship would never work unless he left drugs alone. Curt was famous for staying out all night. One weekend, he didn't make it home at all, so Babe told him to pack up and leave. She had warned him repeatedly, but he ignored her pleas. She knew it wouldn't work, even though she tried to give him the benefit of the doubt.

Keeping Josie's children kept Babe aware of the needs and concerns about them, especially after a neighbor discovered Josie's six-year-old daughter roaming the neighborhood at 5:00 am, crying for her mother, who was not at home. Things were on the verge of a catastrophe, and Babe sensed it. But everyone ignored the warnings. Their sinful habits had blinded them. Their marriage was on the rock, and Josie was speaking death wishes.

Crying out to God became a practice of Babe's even though she didn't feel her place was in the church. She had always known from childhood experience that God listened to everyone that called on his name; she knew she could never turn her back on Josie if she ever needed her. Faithfully, Babe watched her children, taking them to their tutor since their grades were failing. They weren't to blame for a family gone wrong, knowing they weren't responsible.

Josie was still good as gold. Whenever she found a good deal, she kept Babe on her mind. In a conversation one day, Josie asked Babe if she wanted to sell her rent house. It hadn't occurred to Babe, but since there was an offer to be considered, Babe told her money talked and nonsense walked; meaning, it would have to be money only. Babe was aware that junkies sold off homes and anything else in exchange for heroin and cocaine to their dealer.

Babe felt she had to be specific. Since she already had it refinanced, it seemed to be a good way to get from under it.

Arrangements were made to meet at Babe's place in order to talk over the deal with people they knew. Malcolm called Babe up and told her she'd be crazy not to take three ounces of cocaine in exchange for her rented house. Babe was sure then that she would have to rely on them to sell it for her. That would leave room for many problems. Malcolm informed her that she could make three times as much profit.

"Forget it," Babe said.

Later, she agreed on a price for the buyer to assume, and they set a date for closing. Mix feelings surfaced, and Babe regretted selling the house, especially since the buyer was associated with drugs also. But the fact that it was all legal made it hard to rule out. The tenant was notified that the house would be sold.

Josie and Malcolm couldn't wait to hear from Babe, hoping she would consider going in on a deal with them. Constantly, she reminded them that she didn't want that kind of business. Babe couldn't believe they were still denying that drugs were a waste of money, everything goes up in smoke and then your soul. She regretted that they were involved in drugs.

One day she searched the papers and noticed the apartment classified ads. There were so many nice ones near where she worked; she could rent her house easily since the interest rate was low. Babe thought maybe she was glad she hadn't been able to buy the house she really wanted. She placed an ad in the paper in hopes of renting her house.

Later that day, Babe told Josie what she had done. Josie said she felt like she was losing her only friend. Babe assured Josie that she could always count on her, no matter where she lived. But for the sake of her sanity and perseverance, she wanted and needed a change of location.

Prayers went forth every day that her house would rent fast so she could escape the influence she was under. Babe listed several different sources with no results; she became discouraged.

Although she was tired and scared of the involvement, still she found she had an irresistible urge to take advantage of the dope when she could. The fact that Babe had a clean record, and she didn't want to be caught up in anything illegal, made her reluctant to be involved with them.

Josie joked about her customers going to the rehabilitation center for help, but then coming right back to her again. Babe was hurt at how cold Josie had grown.

After dinner one evening, Malcolm began to joke about the crucifix Babe sported around her neck. He told her that she either had to be hot or cold or God would spit her out. Babe knew that was scriptural because she had heard it before. It didn't matter to her at that moment since she had never taken much time to understand half the scriptures in the Bible.

Babe responded to Malcolm, "I can still believe in
   God."

Josie started in on her, saying she could never go back to that way of living.

"But I don't want to be blind forever," Babe said.

And that started Babe to think just how lost they really were, and she was caught up in the middle of it all.

No one ever answered the classified ad to lease her house, so Baby just dealt with it. Josie still had a key to her place, so it wasn't unusual to find her at the house when Baby came home from work. Babe could tell she wasn't feeling well. This was the second bout with sickness Josie had experienced. The first resulted in a trip to the hospital because of a severe kidney infection.

Josie was famous for pushing herself in order to meet financial obligations. At times, she would work all night selling drugs. Babe felt relieved when she had found others to work with her rather than herself. Babe was more trouble to her than good. The sight of a police officer frightened her, and everything in the air seemed to be following them or, at least, that's what she thought. Josie had a sinus problem that wouldn't clear up because of the intake of cocaine she was using. There were other problems as well. Babe suggested she go to the hospital for a while, and she would keep the children until she was better. One doctor told her she needed surgery, but Josie refused to consider the thought of being hospitalized.

She continued to work around her physical problems.

Chapter 8

Family Ties

It wasn't normal for relatives from out of town to visit since the Johnsons weren't a close-knit family. When the news arrived, that Jonni was in town and staying with Uncle Will, all the girls decided to visit. Jonni had left Tulsa and relocated to Michigan over twenty years ago when her mother divorced Uncle Will. Uncle Will tended to be somewhat of a Casanova; he wasn't faithful in his first marriage, and after both families divorced, it was hard for the family to keep up with family ties. Uncle Will, who was Patrick's father, lived with his girlfriend. He had been married twice and was living together out of wedlock with a lady friend now.

Uncle Will's daughter, Jonni, and her husband had come from Muskegon, Michigan, to visit. Jonni and Josie were the closest cousins when they were growing up and had twin names. Jonni had married a preacher and had two children. When she learned her father was living in sin, she insisted that her husband officiate at his wedding. They arranged the private wedding in her father's home.

The evening of the wedding, Candi, Josie, and Babe loaded all the children and attended the wedding. It was small and private, but nice. Jonni didn't know what Josie's life was like, and it was like no one wanted to volunteer that kind of information.

Jonni was as beautiful as ever, with a certain glow about her. They all chatted about old times, and suddenly, Babe thought about Patrick, Uncle Will's son and Jonni's brother. When Babe mentioned him, Jonni had never heard about him and wanted to know more. Babe told her as much about him as she could; Patrick hadn't met everyone in the family.

Uncle Will walked out of the room while Babe was telling Jonni about Patrick, and Babe couldn't help but wonder if she had put her foot in her mouth. Before leaving, they all exchanged phone numbers and addresses in order to keep in touch.

Babe promised to send pictures of Patrick to Jonni.

Later that evening at home, Babe thought about how Uncle Will left the room when she started talking about Patrick, as if she had said the wrong thing because of how Uncle Will responded. But it seemed unfair for him to deny his fatherhood to Patrick.

A month later, Patrick was in town again. He knew Susan, a friend of Josie; he had her convey a message to Josie. Soon they had planned a get together at Babe's house for dinner. Patrick had not changed. His slim appearance indicated he hadn't slowed down. Patrick showed pictures of his son, who lived out of town with his girlfriend, who was somewhat connected to a celebrity singer. Patrick hadn't been married nor did he speak of getting married. Yet through the conversation, it was like Babe could detect a spirit of deception. She didn't care one way or the other, but she began to wonder what he was trying to hide.

Babe's main concern was that Patrick meets his sister, whom he'd never met. While they sat talking, Babe dialed Jonni's number, and Patrick and Jonni talked for a good thirty minutes. Babe felt such joy in having connected them together. They exchanged addresses and promised to keep in touch.

When Jonni and Patrick finally met over the phone, Babe felt a sense of joy since they had never met. Patrick disappeared afterward; he was too busy to keep in touch, and after Babe saw that Patrick was into cocaine like Josie and Malcolm, she knew it wouldn't be worth it to keep in touch.

Josie's condition worsened. Her sinus ailment never cleared up, and she was hit with the pressure of Malcolm's decision to quit his job. Malcolm's continuous use of drugs was seriously affecting his lifestyle.

With Josie's health failing and Malcolm going off on deep end, danger was in the air.

One Sunday evening, Josie wasn't feeling her best, and she called Babe over to deliver a package to Joyce. When Babe returned, Josie was still suffering from a sinus infection. Malcolm drove up, complaining about everything. Josie was so fed up with the whole mess; she suggested that she consume the whole bottle of valium tablets sitting on the kitchen table.

That Monday Babe grew weary about Josie's condition and was sick of everything she was going through. She called in to report her absence at work, hoping she could somehow convince Josie to check on her health and to leave the drug scene to Malcolm if he insists on doing it. Instead of accepting any of Babe's advice, Josie lured her into running errands again.

Joyce stopped by and left a few goods in exchange for drugs. Joyce's habit was indeed bad. She was using the needle, which was more addictive. Joyce was leaving and Babe was returning, and their conversation ended as though Joyce was coming back later.

Since the kids had missed sessions with the tutor, Josie suggested Babe pick them up from school and take them to the tutor. On the way there, Babe's car was giving her problems. She called Papa at the tutor's home. After failing to reach him, Babe called Josie to come and pick them up. Because of the commotion, they weren't able to make the tutor session. Babe left her car at the tutors, and they went to Josie's house. Again, Babe tried to talk with Josie, but company was present; it was not the right time to talk to Josie. Josie told Babe to take her new car since her car was still stranded at the tutor's. Babe had been off work for two days and would need a car to get there.

At home that evening, Babe located her papa and asked him to check on her car. He said he would later on that week. While stretched out on the couch that night, Babe lay staring at the ceiling, thinking about Josie and all she was going through. Babe knew she was tired of trying to keep her family together. She was breaking laws, getting further from the truth, but she was still holding on.

How Strong She Must Be, Babe thought.

"God, I wish I was that strong," Babe prayed, hoping God would hear her and know her heart because she really felt lost for words. Babe feared the sin she was in had separated her from God.

It was two in the morning, and the ringing of the phone awakened Babe; it was Mother, and Babe could barely understand Mother, for her crying. Josie had been rushed to the hospital by Life Flight. Mother was mumbling through her sobs. Someone had badly beaten Josie. Mother needed Babe to pick her up and take her to the hospital. Quickly, Babe dressed and was thankful to have Josie's car. The roads were empty, without a single car to hold up traffic. As Babe sped across town to the hospital, she thought of Malcolm and how they had been arguing; she prayed he hadn't done anything foolish.

Mother and Babe arrived at the hospital. Papa and Candi were already there. They sat in the private waiting room where the doctor met them and told them Josie's condition was critical. They needed to begin surgery right away. Since Malcolm was at the police station for questioning, Mother signed the release for the surgery.

Before the doctor left, he asked if anyone wanted to see Josie before they took her to surgery.

Babe stepped forward, softly speaking, "I do."

Her head was bandaged, and the nurse explained that a part of her skull was broken, and vital parts of the brain were exposed. They gave her a 20-percent chance to survive, and if she did live, she would be a vegetable. Babe leaned over and gave Josie a kiss before they rolled her off for surgery. Babe could hardly believe that only a few hours earlier, she was talking to Josie.

Many family members were at the hospital; Babe decided to go on to work. She had already been off two days, and the thought of waiting would only frustrate her. Her best remedy was to always stay busy after an upsetting experience.

Babe went directly to work and arrived early. Since she was the first person there, she had plenty of time to cry to God. Her memory flashed back to what Josie had said last Christmas. "There's usually a death soon after a family comes together."

"Dear God," she prayed, "please, not Josie."

Tears ran down Babe's cheeks. No matter how hard she tried to hold them, she had a strange feeling that this was the end for Josie. The only one who could help her was God. Inwardly, Babe pleaded for God's mercy and grace to spare her life, hoping he would turn it around for good.

A coworker came in and asked Babe how she was feeling, somewhat shocked to look into the coworker's face because Babe's face was swollen, and tear stained. Babe knew it would be difficult to share the story.

After she explained what had happened, the coworker patted her shoulder and said she would explain to the supervisor so she wouldn't have to repeat the details. Babe thanked her. Early that morning, they called her from the hospital. The surgery was completed, but Josie's blood pressure had dropped. She started hemorrhaging while in surgery. Suddenly, Babe realized it was better to pray for God to have mercy on her soul more than anything. Babe's mother wanted her there with the rest of the family. Babe told her supervisor how critical the situation was and that she needed to return to the hospital.

All the family was at the hospital; the three brothers out of town were notified and were due to arrive any day now.

At the hospital, everyone was huddled together or was pacing the floor. Josie was placed on a life-support system and wasn't expected to live long. Babe didn't know what kind of support they expected from her; she was barely holding on herself.

Babe's mother told her that the doctors thought they had lost her on the operating table. Mother cried in Babe's arms.

"If she's still unconscious in seventy-two hours, Malcolm has the right to disconnect her from the life-support system and sign the death certificate."

After several hours, they allowed the family to see Josie in intensive care. Her unconscious body lay there, stiff and bandaged. They had cut all her hair off for the surgery, and her body was swollen and covered with dark bruises. She looked nothing like herself.

As Babe left the room, she thought of Josie's three children. Everyone left knowing there was nothing they could do but wait and pray. Babe didn't want to go home; she felt uncomfortable there. It was as if her papa could tell, so he stepped over and asked her to follow them home, and they could check on her car the next day. Her papa invited her to pack a few things and stay with them until the end of the week. Babe had never spent much time with her father and stepmother, but now they spent the evenings talking about Josie. They had not been aware of Josie's involvement with drugs.

Thursday, Babe went to work and had lunch with Cherry, who was a born-again believer. Babe told Cherry about their involvement with drugs. Cherry and Babe had known each other since they were kids. When Babe asked Cherry if she thought maybe, she was reaping what she had sown because she killed the rapist, Cherry explained that her sister was dealing with Satan in the involvement with drugs and that Satan came to kill, steal, and destroy her life.

"Sometimes, if we are not walking with the Lord, he will allow things to happen because we've rejected him," Cherry said.

Cherry told Babe to go to the hospital and speak to Josie as though she were alive and command her to live in the name of Jesus, praying that she would be a living testimony. Babe thought about how Malcolm and Josie chastised her about wearing her cross, as Babe recalled Josie's refusal to seek God's way anymore.

Lunch was a blessing even though Babe couldn't eat. Cherry's counsel was a great help. At work, Babe continued to stay busy and prayed at the same time that God would let Josie live to become a living testimony.

"I'll help her to go the right way, Lord, please have mercy on her soul at least." The thought of going to the hospital and speaking to Josie scared the wits out of Babe. Babe never thought she had a scared streak in her until it came to this.

After work, Babe headed straight to her dad's house, hoping they would see Josie later, then she could pray for Josie the way Cherry instructed her. But she found out her father was checking on her car and didn't come home until late, so they never made it to the hospital.

Finally, two brothers from Dallas made it in, then the other one came from Los Angeles. The seventy-two hours on the life-support system had elapsed, and Malcolm had the legal right to have the system disconnected. They wanted to hold on, but hope was dim.

On Friday, November 22, 1985, at 9:00 P.M., the assisting nurse prayed a prayer of salvation before disconnecting Josie from the life-support system and pronounced Josie legally dead. The immediate family included all of Josie's sisters and brothers and parents and Malcolm; his family preferred not to enter, yet everyone wept frantically when they realized that Josie had been disconnected from the life-support system and there was life no more in her. It was two days before Josie's thirty-fifth birthday.

Malcolm came out of the room, weeping, and reached for Babe, but she couldn't comfort him; she was bitter because he had started all this mess with drugs, which brought danger into his home.

Babe gently pushed Malcolm away to avoid a confrontation and leaned against the wall, weeping. One by one, family members came out of the ICU.

Malcolm couldn't handle plans for the burial, so his mother did it for him. A small graveside service would be held the following Tuesday.

Back at Pappa's, they discussed Josie's death further. The last they had heard; a man went to purchase some drugs. This man had been told that he was not welcome there because of the way he conducted himself, but Josie let him in. That's when he brutally beat her with a tire tool and escaped with drugs and money.

It seemed strange that Josie would even allow him in her house. Malcolm suspected that someone else was with the junkie, who was an accomplice. Malcolm was the one who found her when he came in late that night. He had another friend with him.

Saturday, Babe returned Malcolm's car and saw the children. Malcolm's mother was keeping them. The children's minds were shattered with confusion. Josie's little girl ran into Babe's arms, crying that she wanted her mother. The night of the murder, they saw their mother lying in a pool of blood, with part of her head and skull crushed. The memory was still vivid as she asked if her mother's head hurt.

After making sure the kids were alright, Babe talked with Malcolm's mother.

"I'm ready to go to church now, one that would be right for me."

"That's good," she said.

Babe embraced the kids before she left and told them how to get hold of her if they ever needed anything. They all cried and hugged one another before leaving.

Sunday would have been Josie's birthday. Since Malcolm's family didn't acknowledge special dates like that, the family didn't even remember. But all Babe could think of was how sad it was to die before your birthday and not know whether you will be going to heaven.

The loss of an immediate family member allowed an employee automatically three days off at work. Babe thanked God because it was a difficult experience she was facing. Josie's death was affecting her worse than people realized; she thought it should've been her in that grave. Josie had everything to live for—a family and a husband—then Babe realized maybe she didn't have all those things to live for, especially if it continued the same way. Something else would have happened. Babe still felt that Josie should've lived long enough to see her children grow up and have grandchildren. It seemed like Babe wouldn't have missed any of that since she didn't have any children.

Malcolm's mother made all the funeral arrangements, and Babe prepared the obituary for print. The week after the burial was Thanksgiving. Since the family was still in town, Babe's mother asked her to prepare Thanksgiving dinner. Babe dreaded preparing a big family dinner; she couldn't find much to be thankful for. But within a couple of days, she realized she couldn't continue to be sorrowful, so she agreed to prepare dinner.

Everyone knew that Josie was the expert cook in the family and Babe was only her helper. Yet the dinner was so good everyone was sure that Josie had passed on her cooking abilities to Babe. Malcolm brought the kids over. To see them break their tradition to join the family that day made it all worthwhile.

Going back to work helped Babe put the past behind her. It was no secret how her sister died, and her coworkers were comforting with words of encouragement and love. Babe used to call Josie every morning at work to wake her up; that was a habit that was hard to break, and she caught herself dialing the number only to hear it repeatedly ring.

Babe found it difficult to stay in her own house. A second attempt was made to lease it. James, her oldest brother from California, was staying a while longer than the other brothers since his job wasn't as pressing. James stayed with Babe, and she thought it would work out fine if James decided to stay on, but

James didn't want to work while he stayed; he just wanted to run around with his old high school buddies.

When Babe and her mother realized that James wasn't going to seek out a job while he stayed, they decided to chip in on his airfare since that was another reason why he hadn't left.

Finally, Babe's prayers were answered when a young lady answered her ad to rent her house. Babe had moved some of her clothes over her mother's and stayed with her when she didn't feel like staying there.

Now that Babe was going to lease her house out, she decided to stay with her mother until she found an apartment out south. Every night, Babe wondered about the children, wondering if Malcolm could take care of them. He was still involved in drugs and needed to get his life straightened out.

Babe thought about Josie's request before she died, about keeping her children if anything ever happened to her. All she could think of was to commit to what she told Josie. The thought of raising three kids left Babe worried and concerned. Babe called Malcolm's mother and told her she would be glad to keep the two smallest children as soon as she found an apartment big enough and she could keep the oldest since he stayed with them most of the time anyway. She thanked Babe and said if Malcolm approved of it, she would consider it.

Malcolm must've thought the invitation was for all of them; he called Babe and asked her if he could stay with her since he felt uncomfortable staying at his home after what happened to Josie.

It was the only way she could prove to Josie she wanted to help. Malcolm was making it mighty difficult. Without hesitation, Babe refused Malcolm's offer since she knew he was still involved in drugs and the very fact that he was a brother-in-law made her uncomfortable. Babe hadn't even know that Markie was missing assume dead, after talking to Malcolm about keeping the children, he never told Babe anything it was mother that told Babe about Markie, Mother said that the policemen said it was too deep to deal with all the circumstances behind Markie's disappearance, yet Malcolm never said one word about it. Babe was so upset to hear that.

New Year's Eve was a quiet moment spent listening to fireworks from a bedroom window and sipping a glass of wine. It was a time of peace and New Year's resolution. As Babe fought the urge for drugs, sympathetically, she cried that the craving would leave.

"God, deliver me," she moaned, as she restricted herself to solitary confinement. The fact that she wasn't around the environment made the most difference. It didn't take long before the urge to do drugs disappeared, and the people that did drugs were never around.

Malcolm got back with Babe, letting her know he didn't want to separate his children, so his mother ended up with them. Babe knew it was a blessing that he didn't want them separated. It would have been more than a notion raising two kids already set in their ways.

A day didn't go by that Babe would not think about them, crying out to God that he would shield them with his love and protect them with his peace.

After the New Year, Babe remembered she had agreed to go to church. Staying with Mother was the best thing she could have done. Her mother was a great inspiration in directing her to church as well. Babe didn't want to attend her mother's church, but she was open to her mother's suggestion about a new church on the south side. This church on the south side was growing by leaps and bounds. Babe thought the least she could do was try it out.

The second Sunday in January, they made it to an evening service. It was different, and Babe could tell. It was nondenominational, with a mixture of races. From the very beginning, Babe was intrigued. She had heard that variety was a spice of life, and the variety there was beautiful.

The songs sung brought tears to her eyes. The congregation stood up for about an hour, praising God. That took some getting used to. People were singing and dancing. The music was upbeat, with a soulful expression. After singing the praise songs, the congregation was invited to shake someone's hand or hug them. Babe withdrew, hoping no one would discover her, but several people embraced her with hugs and handshakes until it didn't matter that she touched them. It seemed to relieve her of past hurts.

The sermon was about being obedient to God. What the preacher said seemed real and made sense. After preaching, he asked if anyone needed the strength to be obedient, and if so, to raise a hand. At that time, Babe thought, *what is it like to be obedient? Was it really what I Wanted?*

Before she knew anything, she felt an urgency to thank God for all she had lived through, and if it was time to be obedient, she wanted that for her life now.

Still a little reluctant, she slightly raised her hand, hoping no one would see her. Then the minister asked those who raised their hands to please come to the altar. Babe knew she had to go or become a liar. Hesitantly, she sat there deciding whether to go or not. The scripture said if you're ashamed of Jesus before men, he'll be ashamed of you before the father. The words were so loud in her thoughts that she jumped up and told her mother that she had to go.

Babe's mother knew she was scared; she stood also to follow behind her. At the altar, a feeling of peace covered the area as the preacher prayed for those standing and for others that needed prayer.

Upon returning to their seats, they were asked to hug someone before leaving. Mother and daughter both embraced and repeated a phrase from the song:

"I have a feeling everything's going to be alright."

Chapter 9

Being a Living Testimony

After a couple of visits at church, Babe felt a need to rejoice in the Lord over the new directions her life had taken. Finding a good church made a difference; the little church Mary told her about didn't compare to the one she was attending now.

Babe knew she would be moving out south as soon as she found an apartment, and a church in the same area would be more convenient.

Babe felt good about church and wanted to get her entire life on the right track. She placed another ad in the paper, and pronto, a tenant came to her rescue. Immediately, the tenant wanted to move in. She was on the government-housing program with two daughters. After all the preliminaries were handled Babe had to downsize because she was moving into a smaller apartment again, and she knew all too well that she would have to get rid of some of the things she had. What Babe couldn't sell, she got rid of by either donating or giving to someone in need.

Since Babe didn't want to be rushed, she decided to store her things in storage until she found an apartment comfortable to her needs. That way, Babe could stay with her mother while sorting through her decisions.

Mother stayed in the same neighborhood, and some of the neighbors were still there. Glenda, one of Babe's best buddies had lost contact, but she ended up doing time in jail for some kind of vandalism at her job. Babe had heard about it but didn't know the details. Then several years after she got out of jail, she had a heart attack and died, at the age of forty-three. Babe was devastated after hearing about Glenda's death since they were really close back in the days. Glenda's mother had already died, and it must have taken a toll on Glenda as well.

Babe knew that she had to search for an apartment. As she began looking in the area where she worked, she remembered the apartments directly across the street from the church. They were newly built and had a taste of elegance and luxury, but that always added up to expensive, so Babe decided not to even check them out. There were several apartments near her job, but Babe was undecided as to where to move.

One evening after work, Babe decided to check out some apartments. A couple of miles down the street were some apartments called the Lounge. They seemed to be older because they had been there awhile. They gave Babe a tour of a model apartment that had a den with a bedroom. It was nice, and Babe appreciated the extra room. She was preparing to give a deposit to hold the apartment when she decided to check out the one across the street since neither had a washer and dryer.

Babe asked a receptionist where she could find an apartment in the same area with a washer and dryer or the necessary hookups. The receptionist described two different apartments, one Babe could remember because it was named after a street, and she drove to it first. When she looked at the apartments, they were nice and had everything a person needed, but they were quite expensive. Babe knew the place was too high for her.

It was getting late, and Babe couldn't remember the name of the other apartment the receptionist had told her about, so she asked the receptionist at these apartments for the apartments in the area that would have a washer and dryer. When the lady mentioned Creekwood, it rang a bell, and Babe remembered it was the name of the other apartments. Quickly, she left to find Creekwood Apartments before they closed, and according to the directions she took, she was directly across the street from the church she had been attending.

Babe remembered how she shunned the thought of moving across the street because they seemed expensive, but actually Babe was surprised to discover that these apartments were only five dollars more than what the ones with the den. It had a built-in microwave, fireplace, and washer and dryer, not to mention the Creekwood Apartments had a Jacuzzi and workout room. It was a total shock to realize there was only a five-dollar difference.

Her mind was made up, and to think that maybe God had something to do with it all made Babe even more excited. Anxious to share the news with her mother, Babe rushed home to start packing as well. Payday was that Friday, and it was planned that Babe would move then. Babe's mother was glad that she found a place to move into; she was happy if Babe was happy.

After Babe got moved in, she noticed how convenient it was to attend church more regularly, and she actually enjoyed it. She eventually joined the church.

Even though she found herself wanting to find another outlet, it seemed like the church was the only door that opened.

The church services were great, but Babe wanted to keep a distance and avoid the holier-than-thou attitudes. Since it seemed like her life was back on an even keel, now seemed like the best time to begin considering outside activities.

Working part time was always a good resource for Babe; she began to apply at several department stores without any success.

Yet a desire to know God was stronger now than before. Going to church really settled Babe's spirit, and she looked forward to Sunday morning and evening service.

Staying across the street from the church led to more regular visits. The excitement at the church was that the minister was single and still young enough to arouse most of the single women that attended the church, not to mention there was an abundance of fellowship. It wasn't long before Babe began meeting friends and volunteering for other areas of the church. She felt her worries were behind her, and she had God to thank. She slept better just knowing her sister's children were in responsible hands. Their grandparents were Jehovah's Witnesses. But Babe figured it was something good in every faith, and she felt there was something to learn in every denomination. As long as she continued to pray for God's direction in their lives, she knew he would be faithful in caring for them.

Life's destiny began to change for Babe as she slowly opened up to God's better plan for her. Going to church wasn't as bad as she had expected and finding an area to volunteer in church gave Babe something to do.

The thought of serving God wasn't quite a reality until one morning, about 3:00 A.M. While Babe slept, an audible voice awakened her. The voice gently and clearly said, "You will be my living testimony."

Babe was alarmed at what it could have been. Then she remembered the prayer her friend suggested she pray for Josie— that she be a living testimony. Babe sat in bed, trying to figure it out, wondering if it could have been God while half hoping that it wasn't God because she didn't know what she could ever do for him when she was feeling inadequate.

A week went by, and Babe was afraid to tell anyone about her experience for fear they would think she was cracking up.

One day at work, Babe was walking with a friend during their lunch hour, and Babe decided to share her experience. Betty laughed and said, "That only happens to movie stars."

Since the idea of preaching didn't quite turn Babe on, Babe was relieved when she said that, now hoping she could convince herself the same.

Only a couple of days later, Babe was sitting up in bed early in the morning, about to get ready for work. Without a thought on her mind, again she heard an audible voice say, "They need to know!"

Babe's eyes lit up with astonishment, and her heart rejoiced with laughter to know that God had actually spoken to her. Babe truly knew that she knew God had chosen her.

At work, she couldn't restrain the joy from bubbling over, and her relationship with God began to take on a new meaning. Babe was the first employee at work, so when the others came in, they stopped by her office. Janice came by and asked how she was doing. Excitedly, Babe bounced up and down in her chair and clapped her hands.

"I'm going to work for God," Babe told her.

"If you're not careful, you're going to the funny farm," she answered with a smile on her face and moved on. Joyfully, she sat thinking, *God actually spoke to her.*

Janice and Betty liked the new change in Babe. In the days to come, Babe realized the thrill of hearing God's voice was behind her if she didn't know what God wanted her to do. Babe realized that she didn't know herself what to tell people about God. She had always believed in her own way, and that was enough for her, yet the Word of God states that even devils believe and tremble. To think that Babe was just as bad as the devil if she didn't do what the Bible said, that left her wondering how many more blind people the devil was tricking. It seemed like the short time Babe had been in church rekindled things she had learned, especially when scriptures came to her mind fast enough to answer her thoughts. Scriptures from the Bible began to convince Babe like never before.

"Harden not your heart when you hear the word of God."

Doubting thoughts occurred as she struggled with what she should do. It seemed that either way, Babe was doomed, knowing how much she feared God. Thinking back, when God pulled her through countless trials, regardless of her fears, she knew she couldn't betray him now.

Once again, God's Word reminded her that not only was God a god to be feared, but he was a god of love, and through God, you can do all things, for it's he who strengthens you.

According to the world standard, Babe didn't consider herself a super-bright person, just someone that worked hard and enjoyed being around people. She thought back to the special-education class she attended in elementary school, and how even now, the college courses overwhelmed her at times. But the Bible seemed to be a book of a different story; she was really interested in biblical history and how the love of God was shed abroad. Even though she considered herself slothful at times, she could already tell God's power was doing a work for her. God would also have to strengthen her because of some habits she wasn't quite sure she wanted to give up. The fear of being single for the rest of her life scared her. Babe had heard about some holier-than-thou lifestyles, and it all seemed like a bunch of bondage. She didn't want to be a hypocrite, preaching one thing and doing another, so she asked God to help her to do his will.

This church was one of a kind. The pastor was single, and a lot of single women attended there for that reason only. Many felt that the pastor would be their husband. It appeared a spirit of deception was at the church because they had heard a voice indicating that they would marry the pastor. Frankly, Babe didn't see anything special about him other than the fact that he was funny at times and preached a good sermon. She knew the women were drawn to him by his money and status, and he got the money from them, so that didn't prove anything. But as Babe thought about these things, she heard a voice say, "You can have him."

Babe wasn't sure that she even wanted him as a husband until she started to wonder if this was God's will for her to marry a preacher. Knowing that time would tell, she decided to carry on with the things of God until everything came together.

Everyone at church seemed to be living a somewhat straight life. Some Babe had met prior to church life, and she knew they were nothing but stiff necks. Others had been in church for so long, it was nothing more than religion to them instead of a relationship with God. Babe felt free from sin, delivered from herself and ready to win souls for the kingdom.

At church, they started on this testimony stuff. It was hard to believe what some people would share; they shared everything God had ever done for them.

One girl shared that she had been raped and was haunted by the rapist repeatedly until authorities finally caught him. The agonizing trial resulted in a forty-year sentence for the rapist. How courageous of her to share that before a large crowd. Babe felt the eyes of the people on her and wondered if God would ever want her to share her past. As she sat quietly, an impression in her spirit spoke and said, "The lost sheep."

Babe had already met people at the church that used to work in the nightclub with her, and she figured, with the help of Melody, the Word about her past had already hit the surface. Melody was also in the drug scene when Malcolm and Josie were circulating it. Of course, Melody had worked with Babe in the nightclubs, and she knew that Babe was quiet-spoken and reserved, not involved in anything rowdy or anything to promote trouble.

It was later found out that Malcolm and Melody got together after Josie's death and became a couple. Maybe that's why Melody didn't continue her fellowship at the church. It seemed that people could identify Babe wherever she went.

One weekday at church, Babe listened to the pastor as he looked directly at her, stating that they prayed for some people to come to that church. Babe thought perhaps, he meant after the rape and the justifiable homicide prayers were sent forth for her. *Amazing,* she thought, because she never let the situation get her down, and all the prayers that went forth to God on her behalf made her very thankful.

Suddenly, Babe realized the reason why the people prayed was because God prompted them to, and he would ultimately receive all the glory.

Six months after Josie died, Jonni was murdered by a man who said God told him to kill her. The news was devastating, and Babe couldn't understand since Jonni was living a Godly life, but the scriptures comforted Babe as she read, "Where it will reign on the just and the unjust." Babe wondered if Josie needed a guide to show her the light, and since Jonni died in Christ, she might have had to help Josie.

Reservation and fear rose within Babe as she thought back on what her past was like, knowing there were some things that would be hard to understand about her. She found it near impossible to share it all.

At work, she found herself crying in private as the old her died in order that the will of God could be done in her life. Babe not only believed for the sake of believing; she knew there was a love for God within that she never knew how to express.

"Oh, God, thank you for saving me." All this time, Babe never truly knew how much God loved her because she was too busy trying to do it her way.

After work one evening, in her apartment clubhouse, Babe was relaxing in the spa where she met a young girl in the sauna. Babe felt led to witness to her about Jesus. She told Babe that her brother, who was only thirteen, had spoken in tongues. Babe explained that the people in her church spoke in other tongues also, but she hadn't yet.

"It's in the Bible, so I believe it's of God when it's done properly."

She listened as Babe shared her faith in God, then she expressed how she dreamed of being married to her boyfriend, whom she lived with. Babe advised her to go to college and stay in church, and God would direct her life if she let him. They went their separate ways, and that audible voice within her spoke, "Fishers of men."

The spirit of God reminded her again of his commission to everyone.

At church they talked about fasting a lot. The pastor had fasted thirty days for his thirtieth birthday, consuming nothing but fruit juices. He said the Holy Spirit spoke to him clearly, and as time went on, the spiritual gifts manifested within his life. It all sounded exciting, and Babe wanted to fast, but it seemed hard enough just to diet.

One day, Babe had her mind made up and decided to fast. All day, Babe meditated on God's Word, and when she got home that evening, she snacked on popcorn and soda pop and prayed to God that his will be done in her life, and then she read the Bible all evening.

The next day after praying, Babe glanced at herself in the bathroom mirror and directed a statement to God. "How I'd love to hear from you, God, just a word of encouragement."

Within her heart, she heard a voice speak, "Faith,"

Surprised, Babe's eyes sparkled, and she asked, "Is that you, God?"

He didn't say a word, but somehow, she knew before the day was over, she would get a confirmation.

At work, Babe kept a daily word book on her desk. Upon arrival at work, she flipped open the book to the current day. To her surprise, the topic was *faith*, and the scripture was Luke 1:37: "Have faith in God." Babe praised God and couldn't wait to share with others her experience. They all thought she was funny, so this was just another cute joke to them.

After sharing her experience with one coworker, Babe joked that since God had answered her so fast, next she would ask him where the pot of gold at the end of the rainbow was. Her friends went on her way. Although Babe never asked about the gold, it was still on her mind. As clear as a doorbell, the voice within her spoke, "It's in your heart." With childlike joy, she ran over to tell her friends that the pot of gold at the end of the rainbow was in your heart. Now Babe knew there was something more to fasting.

Fasting became a part of her life. The pounds she had always wanted to lose began to fade away as a result of fasting in addition to spiritual gain, which strengthened her confidence and belief. All the farfetched stories she had heard about in ministries and read in the Bible were not only reality, but that power was still in the authority of believers today. The fact that Satan, the god of the world, has everyone blind by the power of darkness, and people weren't trusting God.

Babe's worries of ever marrying faded as her love for God grew more. She knew that she was married to God, and nothing could separate her from his love.

After fasting for three days, Babe found herself testifying before a small group at a Friday-night prayer meeting. She thanked God for strengthening her to make such a sacrifice. Babe recalled struggling with how difficult it all seemed to deny herself of things that would only result in worldly gain. As she worried about such things, she began to realize that she made it hard herself simply because of her own negative confessions. That revelation made sense, knowing that a person can make the best or worst of a situation; it's all according to that individual, and most of her problems came from listening to Satan-negative thoughts.

Services at church were on Wednesday and Friday night all day Sunday. Eventually, the church took priority over everything. A hunger for God's Word overtook her in her venture to do God's will.

Friday-night service was worth waiting for. At church, a woman of God ministered in a powerful way, operating in various spiritual gifts. The word of knowledge was spoken by

God through her. As she ministered one night, she revealed information regarding a woman's concern about having a child. Her statement quickened Babe's memory of the doctors that diagnosed her condition. Their prediction was that it would take a miracle before she gave birth. That word convinced Babe, but she didn't care about having children at this point; she knew that she couldn't play around in the Lord's house, and it was more of a warning than anything. If it was God's will for her to be a mother, she figured she would leave it to the Highest God.

Witnessing to others required boldness that Babe prayed for daily but working in a secular environment brought about discouragement that Babe battled often. Consecration to God allowed her to hear the spirit of God better.

As she sat on her living room couch in a state of melancholy, God's spirit spoke, "Joshua." Babe remembered that name was in the Bible; she reached for the Bible and began to read the book of Joshua.

The first chapter of Joshua was a good start; Babe read down and stopped. "Be strong and of good courage: Be not afraid, neither be thou dismayed: For the Lord thy God is with thee wherever thou goest." After reading the verse Babe felt uplifted and encouraged in the Lord. God's Word had strengthened her.

Understanding of God's Word was illuminated. As Babe began to grow in grace, she realized how omnipotent God and his

Word were; it was clearly understood that the Word was living and active and sharper than any two-edged sword. It penetrates even to divide soul and spirit, joints and marrow; it judges the thought and attitudes of the heart.

Messages from the pulpit had Babe seeking God for involvement. One Sunday, the pastor's message said that everyone must be doers and not only hearers of the Word.

Thoughts ran rapidly over the things she knew she couldn't do for God. But then an audible thought clearly said, "Prison ministry."

Prison Ministry? Babe thought. That's the last place she wanted to go, and then she remembered the audible voice that spoke, "Lost sheep," and she understood what it meant.

It would be difficult to deny when you know God has directed you and even if it wasn't what Babe wanted but doing the will of God mattered. Babe prayed for God's strength and direction, and she wondered how she could find out more about prison ministry.

Another Sunday went by, and the pastor mentioned different ministries in his sermon when he mentioned prison ministry. Babe listened closely. He gave no details; another closed case she felt.

At work Babe placed herself around committed Christians; one girl named Carol informed her of outside activities to take part in. A retreat was all new to Babe, but it sounded like fun. A group of women got together for a women's retreat at McAlester, Oklahoma. They gathered after work and carpooled, driving down Friday evening just in time for the last meeting.

After the meeting, they met in a hotel room where they discussed everything. Everyone had their prayer language but Babe. Babe didn't worry about it because it seemed like some were gifted with it, and she didn't want to make it seem complex. It took all the fun out of serving God when people would press you since it didn't make much sense to her. Everyone insisted on praying that Babe would receive the gift of tongues. As they prayed, she listened and wondered what to expect. Babe finally got tired and told them she was ready for bed. It was late, and everyone agreed that this was okay with them.

The next day, they had breakfast together before meeting for the workshop they attended. The workshop was good therapy; they learned to release what was on their mind. After the workshop, Babe wanted a break from the hard seats and a time to refresh on her own. She'd planned to skip the afternoon service.

While everyone prepared to leave, Babe had already discovered a sauna in the hotel to relax in. The sauna wasn't very warm, but she didn't care; she just wanted a place to escape to.

Patiently, she waited, hoping the sauna would warm up. A woman walked in and introduced herself. "Hello, my name is

Brenda Penn, I'm here with my husband for the prison ministry convention."

Now it was the third time the prison ministry had been mentioned, and Babe's reaction was somewhat startled. She asked, "How can I learn more about prison ministry? I feel that God is trying to direct me, but I don't know where to start."

Brenda informed Babe that her husband was the director for the Oklahoma County Prison Ministry. She suggested putting Babe on the mailing list to receive a monthly bulletin, announcing Bible studies and committee meetings at various prisons in Oklahoma County.

Babe shared with Brenda about her sister's death. Then Brenda told her about a prisoner who was led to Christ by a family member of the person he had murdered.

Babe's thoughts centered on the guy that killed her sister. He hadn't been arrested yet because he had left town, but charges were filed. There wasn't any remorse in Babe's heart for him, knowing that vengeance belonged to the Lord. Nor did it seem necessary to consider leading him to Christ whenever they caught up with him.

Upon leaving the sauna, Babe couldn't help but think of how God had tied everything together. She knew prison ministry was the ministry he wanted her in.

When the girls came back from the workshop, Babe told them about what happened, and they were astounded. They all left early Sunday just in time to arrive back in Tulsa and attend their own church service.

That evening at church, Babe inquired about prison ministry with an usher. He said he had been involved in it but was now enrolled in Bible college and hadn't the time. A lady nearby overheard and interrupted them. She explained that she had been active for ten years. She had a display of booklets, which she published and distributed in the prisons. Each booklet had her picture and her address on the back. She gave Babe a few booklets and prayed with her, and as they went their separate ways, her acquaintance left Babe wondering if she could write a book since her life was full of testimonies.

Another confirmation was just what she needed. Babe saw the assistant pastor's wife and decided to inquire with her. She informed her that the church supported outside prison ministries. She gave Babe the name and number of one of them.

On the way home, Babe recalled that the church bulletin announced a midnight ministry at a local nightclub. She was curious to know what could be going on at a nightclub since Babe was familiar with the clubs.

At the club the functions didn't begin until midnight, but Babe arrived early enough to meet the girl who had been raped and shared her testimony before the congregation. Babe introduced herself and complimented her for her bravery in sharing her testimony. She worked at the club but also had a desire to work in prisons. Babe explained her interest in prison ministry. Carol introduced her to the manager of the club, who also attended the same church. Her manager was involved in a prison ministry workshop. Babe was astounded at the connections. She practically told them her life history, and they were both shocked at what she had told them.

Around midnight, the band from the church set up, and the group started to play. Babe observed the customers leave while others stayed to hear the Gospel and the testimonies. Church members flooded the club in order to support one another. The Gospel songs stirred everyone's spirit with joy and prepared them to hear the testimony of a young man who had been involved in drugs, selling and using them. His crime caught up with him, and he was sentenced to serve twenty years in prison. His family prayed for him out of prison in three years. Now he's active in a prison ministry himself. Before it was over, Babe had met nearly everyone there.

It wasn't long before she was attending a workshop and orientation on prison ministry. Babe heard about a group that was preparing to go into a correction center for a prison invasion, which would last a whole weekend. It was her first opportunity to experience prison ministry, and she was excited to know she was in the will of God.

In the prison, she met different people and shared Jesus with them. Some received Jesus and others doubted. Babe shared with as many people as she could, realizing that the more she decreased, the more God would increase in her. Opportunities to volunteer in the prisons were infrequent, but Babe soon looked forward to more visits. She received a monthly schedule of committee meetings and Bible studies throughout the Oklahoma County prisons. A couple Babe met through another prison ministry asked her if she would join them in their ministry from time to time.

Nine months had passed since Josie was murdered. Mother had already claimed that they would capture the murderer and justice would be done. Babe never thought much about it, knowing that God would take care of it one way or another. While reading the paper one morning, Babe read that the guy had been located in Arizona and was arrested and was on his way to Tulsa, where he would be tried. Babe immediately called her mother to inform her of the news. She had just finished talking with the detective and already knew. Mother was sure this guy would be caught, and it came to pass.

With the guy accused of killing Josie caught, Babe thought back to what Brenda had told her about a family member leading the accuser to Christ.

At work, Babe found herself pondering on the thought of witnessing to this prisoner. She knew that she had no hard feelings toward him but didn't think it was necessary to confront him directly. She searched for the answer, knowing that God would direct her. Babe prayed to God for directions, and quietly, she listened as that still small voice spoke, "You must do what's right."

Babe had been in church long enough to know what was right. God's Word said that it's not his will that anyone perishes, and he that wins a soul is wise. After realizing how effective this man could be if he stood up for Jesus in prison, the idea of witnessing to him began to make more sense. If he turned his life over to Christ, he would be able to minister in prison.

When he arrived at the county jail, Babe wrote to him. After writing several letters without receiving a response, Babe continued to write out of obedience to God, hoping that God would turn his life around and that he would experience the love of God.

Babe knew he received her letters since they didn't come back to her. She trusted God that he would read them. The man's name was Billy Jones. Babe vaguely remembered Curt having an associate by that name, so she located Curt and questioned him. Curt said that he didn't seem like the type who would do anything like that.

Billy stayed in the county jail for at least six months before his trial. Babe wrote to him at least once a month to let him know she was praying for him.

One day at work, in the mail room, Babe was talking with an employee, and she informed Babe that Billy Jones' brother-in-law worked there. This man, named Barry, was a person Babe talked to nearly every day on his mail run, yet she knew nothing of this.

When he brought in the mail, she confronted him; Barry held his head down in shame and apologized for his brother-in-law. He didn't want Babe to learn of the relationship, but he couldn't deny it. Barry's wife's sister was married to Billy Jones. Then he told Babe that she knew Billy's wife because they graduated from the same high school. Sure enough, Babe remembered attending a few classes with her. She told Barry not to feel bad because all things work together for good for those who loved the Lord.

Babe shared with Barry her involvement with prison ministry and how she had been writing to Billy in jail. Barry told her that he went to see Billy and that he was changing. He was reading his Bible and seeking the Lord. It occurred to Babe then that perhaps she could visit Billy and let him know she was serious.

Babe asked Barry if he could arrange it. Barry agreed to talk with him to see if Babe could be put on the visitors' roll.

Eight months passed before Billy's trial. The attorney and investigators gathered all the evidence and issued subpoenas. Babe wasn't summoned, and she was glad for that. She didn't want to live through the horrible details all over again. Josie had been dead nearly a year, and Babe was living a totally different life.

The desire to do drugs was entirely gone now. Babe was thankful that God saved her to do his will. Malcolm and his father were subpoenaed. The hearing date was rescheduled several times before they went to trial. Babe was kept up on the news by various sources.

The paper published the outcome of the trial, and the verdict was guilty for Billy, and he was given a life sentence. Babe continued to write to Billy, but she didn't receive a letter from him, but one day, Billy decided to write Babe, and to her surprise, both Babe and Billy shared the same birthday. It was interesting to find this out as Billy had someone to help him write a letter to Babe. Babe could see that he struggled with knowing how to write, and all that he said made it all worthwhile to finally hear from him. He stated how sorry he was and that he would be glad to meet Babe.

After the commotion of the trial, Barry informed Babe that Billy had put her on the visitors' registration list. At one time, the thought of witnessing to this guy had seemed far from reality. Now Babe would meet him face-to-face. She felt sure God would express his love for Billy through her. The day arrived for Babe to visit Billy; she brought him several Christian workbooks as a gift.

In the waiting area of the jail, Babe prayed silently until her name was called. The heavy steel doors clanged shut behind her; private compartments behind a framed glass window secured the prisoners. Not knowing what Billy looked like, Babe turned to a guard to ask where he was. It was then Babe noticed a man waving for her attention, and she realized it was Billy.

Telephones outside the glass windows allowed them to communicate with each other. Babe introduced herself to Billy and explained what God had done for her and why she came. Billy was elated as they both talked about Jesus and what he was doing in their lives. Babe told him of the many opportunities she'd received to go into the prisons to minister; she hoped Billy would understand the commission to the whole world.

At first it was difficult for Billy to look directly at Babe, but as they continued talking, a sense of peace came over him, and he was able to express himself. He told her he was sentenced for life, but his attorney said he might be out in ten years.

At first Babe was upset to hear he would be out in ten years with good behavior. Then she had to repent to God, knowing she should be happy for him either way. Babe felt sure Billy could work for the Lord, whether he was in prison or out. Time ran out, and Babe had to leave, but she left the books she had brought for him with the guard.

Halfway to the exit, Babe turned to see Billy watching and waving with a smile on his face; she felt that her visit proved effective, and she had planted good seeds. That evening, she knew the strength of God had lifted her higher than any drug she had ever tried.

Billy would soon be transferred to a maximum-security prison, and she wouldn't be able to write to him anytime soon. The recent visit proved prayer does work.

At church, Babe became busier still. Working with the five- and four-year-old kept her pretty busy. The children were cute and teaching them brought on a real challenge. They asked questions that Babe wouldn't believe their small minds could think of. She found herself studying more, just to keep up with their ingenious little minds. Then she joined the choir. Since the church had three services every Sunday, Babe had a chance to participate in everything.

On Wednesday nights, she worked with the ten- through twelve-year-old girls, which challenged her to study the Word even more.

Time had turned things around, and Babe realized that everything was what a person made of it. She could make the best or the worst of a situation. It was entirely up to her. She loved being active, and it didn't bother her to have a full schedule. Helping people both in the church and outside filled the void in her life. She hadn't realized before how self-centered she had been until she realized how many lost and dying people there were in the world, and the good thing about it all, she didn't miss anything in the world.

Prison ministry activities continued to keep her busy. Another Prison Invasion weekend was coming up, and Babe wasn't sure if she could get off work. Everyone at work had seen the change in her life, so her supervisor didn't hesitate to approve the day off for her.

The volunteers met ahead of time to discuss the details of what to expect. Babe was appointed the photographer. Plans were to leave early Friday morning. They were to stay the weekend at the YMCA and minister at Mabel Bassett, a correction center for women, located a few hours from Tulsa.

Driving time allowed the volunteers to open up and converse with one another about their walk with the Lord. Everyone appeared much older in their faith. Babe wanted to learn from their testimonies. She had always considered herself a believer but didn't know enough about the Bible or serving God; she had been content to believe that he existed. She remembered when she thought she was strange when she found herself praising God for no particular reason, and now, she realized she should have been doing it all along.

They arrived at the YMCA late Sunday night, after settling in. Monday morning, everyone was anxious to get past the guarded electric fence to witness Jesus to the inmates. First, they met with the chaplain, and she reviewed the prison rules they were to follow. Refreshments were served to the volunteers as they prepared their packs with books and Christmas cards to distribute to the inmates, and then they formed teams; Babe was placed with Karen, who seemed mature in the Lord. They witnessed to the residents, who were given less than a year in the minimum-security house. Babe listened to Karen, and soon learned how to suggest prayer when needed.

Good preparations were made, and everyone was ready to give it their best shot. Babe had been warned against taking pictures if the inmates didn't approve. But to her surprise, most of them wanted their pictures taken. After prayer and fellowship, they're invited to the evening service and suggested they bring a friend to the gymnasium for the service.

After the morning mission, the volunteers gathered in the chaplain's office before the evening service started to exchange praise reports and replenished their book supply. Amazing progress had been made. Many women had changed their sexual preference since they're incarcerated, but the witness of the volunteers changed their hearts, and they were led to the Lord. Everyone was looking forward to the evening service. They prayed that the women there would come to God in a personal way, allowing Jesus to be Lord of their life.

That evening, women from the entire correction center gathered in the gymnasium. There were four separate buildings that housed the residents. The unit where Babe witnessed was minimum security.

Babe was advised not to take pictures for the service that evening. While helping people find seats, Babe recognized someone who looked familiar. It was Joyce, Josie's friend that shoplifted and exchanged stolen goods for drugs. Joyce recognized her as well. Babe sat next to her during the service and shared with her how fulfilled her life was without drugs.

Tears ran down Joyce's face; it was such a coincidence to see Joyce, now really going through a change in her life. Babe sensed the spirit of God taking effect. After a few songs were sung, a lady ministered, and there was an altar call. Joyce was the first one to make a move to receive salvation. Counselors waited until the prayer was completed. They gave each lady a packet explaining the new birth. The service lasted two hours in order for the residents to have a security check. That gave them a little time to fellowship. Joyce came over and told Babe she was ready to make a commitment. She asked her to visit her tomorrow in the east house dorm. Babe promised her she would.

That night, it was late before they went to sleep. At the YMCA, some of the volunteers went to a nearby hotel so they could sleep better. At the YMCA, others just sacked out on the floor with sleeping bags.

Time alone allowed Babe to cry out to God, thanking him that Joyce crossed her path once again, and she was able to offer her something better than drugs. Prison ministry wasn't so hard to accept after Babe understood what God meant by the "lost sheep," especially since she was lost in sin many times in her life.

The next morning, the volunteers ate breakfast with the inmates. Sitting with them helped break the distance they felt and established a closer unity. Babe was startled at how many inmates recognized her. Several were high school classmates. Conversation was sparse as Babe tried to think of what to say to them in such an awkward place, maybe mention a class reunion, but Babe didn't attend them, and she didn't think it was appropriate to ask why they were there.

After breakfast, the volunteers met in the chaplain's office where they had praise-and-worship service. Today, Babe was determined to visit Joyce; however, the volunteers decided not to rotate, but to minister to the same people as the day before in order to get better acquainted.

All that day, Babe worried how she would visit Joyce. After ministering to the same girls as the day before, Babe finished with some extra time. It began to sprinkle as she hurried toward the East Dorm. When she arrived, she saw a girl who appeared to be very lonely; she told Babe she was locked up for killing her husband in self-defense and asked for a prayer. After Babe prayed, the girl felt better. When Babe asked her about Joyce, she told her that Joyce was her neighbor, and then she showed her where Joyce resided.

Babe had to wake Joyce, but she didn't mind. The rooms in the East Dorm were like a luxury hotel compared to the dorm Babe had left. The rooms were more private, with walls and doors instead of open space. Since the lobby area was bigger, Joyce led Babe out into the lobby area.

Joyce had gained some weight since the last time Babe had seen her, which was shortly before Josie's death. Joyce explained that she had testified at Josie's trial, and she was sentenced because of a shoplifting case. She then began to share with Babe what had happened the night of Josie's murder.

She explained that night she was going to make a few runs with Josie. Joyce and Billy were together buying drugs. Billy came over to Joyce's house later to find out if Josie was alone. After that, Billy left, and Joyce didn't find out until 4:00 A.M. The morning Josie had been taken to the hospital.

Babe never knew about Joyce's involvement until now. Joyce and Babe both thought it was strange how it all happened. They suspected someone else was involved, but they couldn't quite put it together. Joyce excused herself to go to her room while Babe waited. She brought back some papers, which she presented to Babe. It was the transcript of the trial on paper. Babe didn't go to any of the trials, but the transcript would help her to understand what really happened.

Babe told Joyce that she saw Billy at the county jail; she was shocked. She knew how close Josie and Babe were. Babe explained to Joyce that life was behind her and the work of the Lord was more important to her. Joyce could see that God really made a difference in her life and shared how she wanted to experience what Babe had. Joyce asked many questions concerning salvation. Babe explained that she needed to be patient because God rewards those who diligently seek him.

They talked so long; Babe almost forgot about the service in the gymnasium.

Babe invited Joyce and told her to invite her friends and enemies. Before leaving, they joined hands and prayed. Joyce began to cry, and Babe could see that most of her problem was over.

That night, the residents packed the gymnasium. A local church held the service, and the volunteers were on standby to counsel the new converts.

Back at the YMCA, they packed their bags to leave early Wednesday morning. Babe tried to hold in her testimony, but while packing, she couldn't help but tell Karen.

The transcript was on her mind, and she was bursting to tell someone. When she explained to Karen about the transcript, she didn't believe her until Babe showed her the papers. Karen reached over to take it, but Babe held it back until she agreed not to tell anyone.

On the floor underneath the covers, Karen read the transcript aloud. Babe listened until she couldn't take any more. Babe excused herself to find a hiding place. The transcript brought back memories of how terrible Josie's death had been.

When Babe returned, Karen had finished reading and wanted to discuss it. Babe apologized because she didn't want to discuss it. Karen understood and told Babe she would keep her in her prayers.

On the way back home, the group sang and praised God. Everyone felt that God's will had been done. It has been a wonderful week. The residents at the correction center had received all the volunteers with open arms. Babe shared her testimony with a few of them, and some she promised to write.

Weeks passed before Babe forced herself to read the transcript. The fear of reading it upset her, yet despite her fears, she sat down one evening and embarked upon it.

Listed on the transcript were all the names of those who had testified. Babe tried to fit the puzzle together. Some of the names she had heard Josie mention. One name she didn't recognize and couldn't picture him as anyone she knew, so she decided to call the phone number on the transcript. Willie William was the name on the transcript. Willie thought Babe was a detective. After identifying herself, he remembered her as well. When he told Babe, his nickname was T-Bird, she then remembered him. He was a friend of Malcolm, Josie's husband.

Willie advised Babe to leave the situation alone before she found out something she couldn't handle. After confessing to Willie of her new life in Christ, Babe assured him that she could handle all things with Christ. Willie informed Babe that most of Malcolm's friends were in jail. After their conversation, Babe realized he had a point. "Therefore, if anyone is in Christ, he is a new creature, old things are gone and the new has come, this is from God." Babe was refreshed in her change and hoped to help change others.

Back at church, she met a friend who was involved in street ministry. Joan told Babe that she ministered to winos, prostitutes, and vagabonds by herself. Babe couldn't tell if Joan was crazy or brave to take on a ministry like that by herself.

Babe realized she could use some help, so they agreed to meet after Friday-night service to pray before they went to the Red-Light District, as she called it. At midnight, they arrived at the corner of Cheyenne and Boston, where the homeless and hungry hung out. Babe couldn't imagine Joan going there by herself, but Babe supposed her angels were encamped around her.

Joan stood at the corner of the store while Babe stood in the center. They gave out tracts while talking to the people that walked by. For some reason, Babe captured the attention of the people. Joan said that it was because they thought she was a prostitute. Babe thought perhaps since Joan looked like somebody's grandmother that was the reason, especially since Babe wasn't dressed like a prostitute. Actually, Babe didn't care what they thought; she just wanted to lead them to Jesus.

Babe turned to a young man who received the tract she handed him. He seemed to show some interest as they talked, but then he said it was wrong to push Jesus on people. Babe explained that she wasn't pushing Jesus on anyone; she just wanted to talk to anyone who would listen. Babe realized this guy wasn't interested, so she went to another area to pass out her tracts.

A month later, she was invited to the county jail with a group from the church, where they would minister the Gospel. In the cell tank, the ladies came in for service, and there was a girl who once lived in the same apartments where Babe had lived as a teenager. Another girl came in and recognized her because she had worked at the same oil company as Babe had. Babe didn't remember Carrie, but Carrie explained that she was Billy's cousin and she appreciated what Babe was doing.

Another girl in the back of the room said she saw Josie the night before she was murdered. Another girl who was sitting near the front said she used to buy drugs from Josie.

As the group was leaving, some men from another tank prepared for service. While walking by, Babe noticed an inmate who looked familiar. It was the man at the Red-Light District who had accused her of pushing Jesus on people. Babe stopped to say something to him, but he kept on walking. Babe thought, *If Only He Had Listened.*

Appendix

Most of the verses used from the Holy Bible were from the King James Version, and some New International translations were also used. The Nag Hammadi Library was referenced in some writings because this collection of scrolls discovered in 1945 in Cairo, Egypt, indicated that after the ascension of Jesus, he stayed with his disciples for forty days afterward, teaching them and showing them the ways of the world as opposed to the things of God. Several books have additional warnings of fornication and how to avoid and shun it.

The *Second and Third Epistle of John* by Judith Lieu and edited by John Rich—this book used in this novel proves that the same problems exist during the days of Jesus' ministry. They also revealed too that the process toward acceptance was not a linear one but was made up of many strands; more importantly, they showed that the question of whether some parts of the New Testament are more central than others has been a consistently recurring one and that their avowed purpose lies elsewhere, leaving room for further interpretation. Also, it emphasizes on the Johannine Christianity, which is based on the teaching of Jesus Christ by the apostle John. Clues throughout the Bible give directions for eternal life, and the name given to John's writings,

"Johannine," bears the meaning of eternal life as well. The meaning of the number 9 has an eternal message, which is what the resurrection of Jesus Christ is all about.

John Rich was instrumental in editing some of the Nag Hammadi and the Gospel tradition as well.

The Lost Books of the Bible (Testament 1998 ISBN -0517-27795-6.) The Lost Gospel of Peter, The Forgotten Book of Eden (Alpha House 1927, ISBN 0-517-30886-x, ISBN 1-56459-636-2. The Psalms of Solomon, Testament of the Twelve Patriarchs.

www.ingramcontent.com/pod-product-compliance
Lightning Source LLC
LaVergne TN
LVHW021806060526
838201LV00058B/3256